D0188269

NON-STOP!
London to Scotland Steam

£7

For twenty-six summers between 1928 and 1961, the English and Scottish capitals of London and Edinburgh were connected by a steam-powered express which did not stop anywhere in the 393 miles between these cities. In this picture A4 No. 60029 *Woodcock* heads the 'Capitals Limited' northwards through York in June 1950, on a working known to British railwaymen simply as the 'Non-Stop'.

NON-STOP!
London to Scotland Steam

A.J. MULLAY

ALAN SUTTON
1989

ALAN SUTTON PUBLISHING
BRUNSWICK ROAD · GLOUCESTER · UK

ALAN SUTTON PUBLISHING INC.
WOLFEBORO · NEW HAMPSHIRE · USA

First published 1989

Copyright © A.J. Mullay 1989

All rights reserved. No part of this publication may be reproduced, stored in a retrieval system, or transmitted, in any form or by any means, electronic, mechanical, photocopying, recording or otherwise, without the prior permission of the publishers and copyright holder

British Library Cataloguing in Publication Data

Mullay, A.J.
  Non-Stop! : London to Scotland steam.
  1. Great Britain. Railway services : London
  and North Eastern Railway, history
  I. Title
  385′.0941

ISBN 0-86299-600-7

Library of Congress Cataloging Data applied for

Cover: In 1961, the last year of non-stop operations, No. 60031 *Golden Plover* has only a few miles to go to Edinburgh on the down 'Elizabethan', seen here at Craigentinny. (J.T. Inglis/Colour Rail)

Typesetting and origination by
Alan Sutton Publishing Limited
Printed in Great Britain by
Dotesios Printers Limited

Contents

With all signals 'off' for a clear run through the station, No. 60031 *Golden Plover* slows for the permanent restriction through Peterborough on the up 'Elizabethan', 11 August 1958. Notice the train headboard is now carried on the bottom bracket while the polished front coupling has been correctly hung. Despite the fact the engine is on the homeward leg of the journey there appears to be an unusually large amount of coal remaining in the tender. (J. Davenport)

Introduction

1 May 1928. The scene is Edinburgh's Waverley station a few minutes after 6 p.m. Platform 10, the southern through platform, is packed with hundreds of people, from local dignitaries and railway officials, down to excited schoolboys.

Well before her booked time, an express blasts out of the 1 in 78 up gradient in the Calton South tunnel, whistles proudly and slows for her first stop since leaving London (King's Cross) at ten o'clock. To the cheers of the waiting throng, the 'Flying Scotsman' has completed her first run in her sixty-six-year history non-stop between the capital cities of England and Scotland. The two sets of crew, Driver Blades and Fireman Morris of Gateshead, and Driver Pibworth and Fireman Goddard of London, step down from the footplate where all four have ridden the last few miles in company with Locomotive Inspector Bramall.

The locomotive – it was none other than No. 4472 *Flying Scotsman* herself – had been crewed by two sets of men because of the length of the journey, the Gateshead crew relieving their London counterparts a few miles north of York, after reaching the footplate by way of the innovative corridor tender. When off duty, each crew rode in a specially reserved passenger compartment which, to their embarrassment, had been bedecked with flowers from a female well-wisher!

Greeted by Senior Magistrate Bailie Hay, standing in for the city's indisposed Lord Provost, the men were also congratulated by A.C. Stamer, deputy to Chief Mechanical Engineer Nigel Gresley, and by local managers. Only the latter might have been aware of how near to disaster the run had come. Over the final few miles the footplatemen had been forced to train a cold-water hose on one of the tender axle-boxes to prevent it overheating to an extent where a replacement engine would be necessary, and the publicity value of the day's running tarnished. As soon as it was decently possible to do so, the A1 Pacific was spirited off to Haymarket depot; indeed, it was only after a night of hard work that No. 4472 could be made ready for the return journey the next day.

However, Waverley station was not the only destination for an unprecedented non-stop run that historic May day. King's Cross station greeted the arrival of the up 'Scotsman' with a burst of cheering appropriate to the return home of a victorious army. Railway author George Dow was present in the packed throng which greeted No. 2580 *Shotover* and her two crews, and has recorded his memories of this unique occasion.

After all, how often has a train received this kind of reception, not because of any particular passengers it was conveying, but simply for itself?

Dow was part of an 'enormous' crowd on the arrival platform when a spontaneous volley of cheering burst from thousands of throats as the 'beautiful gleaming green bulk of No. 2580 brought her train to a stand in Platform No. 1'. Apparently the crowds were so great, and their enthusiasm so ebullient, that the LNER's official welcoming party had great difficulty in fighting their way through to the engine to congratulate the crew.

But this was not, despite the reception given to the two trains, the beginning of non-stop running between London and Scotland. Only the previous Friday, the LNER's rival company, the LMS, had pre-empted the 'Flying Scotsman's' record-breaking non-stop run by operating two expresses from Euston to the twin cities of Glasgow and Edinburgh, each clocking up a distance longer than the LNER's. Yet the LMS had no corridor tenders to make crew relief possible; its was a one-off feat of endurance.

The pirates of the West Coast had stolen the blue riband of non-stop running; how the East Coast men won it back is part of a fascinating story which extended into the 1960s.

Two unlikely locations, both far-flung, played a vital part in the story of British non-stop express operation. The first was a quiet marsh on the North Wales coast between Colwyn and Conway, the second the living-room of Nigel Gresley's home in London's northern suburbs.

Now preserved in its double-chimney form, A4 No. 4498 *Sir Nigel Gresley* nears the end of of its southbound journey as it passes New Southgate with the non-stop 'Flying Scotsman' on an unknown pre-war date. (Photomatic)

It was at Mochdre on the Chester–Holyhead line of the London and North Western Railway that the world's first water-troughs were laid in 1860. These were positioned between the running rails to permit a steam locomotive to refill its tender by means of a simple scoop, using the train's velocity of around 50 mph to propel water into the tank. Like all good ideas it was straightforward in concept and execution, and was patented by John Ramsbottom of the LNWR.

It was to become a vital and integral part of British railway operation in the age of steam, and even slightly afterwards, as it was not unknown for some early diesel types to copy their steam predecessors in topping up their heating boilers in this manner. The first troughs themselves, however, were less permanent, being taken up and relaid at nearby Aber on the same main line some eleven years later, and this latter location is often given as the first to see the laying of railway water-troughs.

The other location to feature in the history of non-stop running was Sir Nigel Gresley's own living-room at Camlet House, Hadley Wood. One evening around 1927 one of his daughters found the stoutly-built 51-year-old Chief Mechanical Engineer of the London & North Eastern Railway crawling along the carpet, through a narrow space between the room's armchairs placed against the wall. To his daughter's reasonable enquiry as to what he was doing, Gresley replied, perhaps not entirely to her satisfaction, 'If I can get through this, my largest engineman can!'

For this domestic experiment convinced Gresley that the corridor tender was a practical means of connecting a locomotive cab to the train itself. By the 1920s, the steam

A4 No. 60034 *Lord Faringdon* coasts through Eryholme on the up 'Capitals Limited' in August 1949. Five years later, this locomotive took part, with *Mallard*, in a unique double 'Non-Stop' run between the capitals. (Photomatic)

locomotive's ability to run more than 300 miles non-stop was not the only crucial factor in considering such long-distance express running. A recent reduction in the number of footplate hours worked by crewmen was a welcome measure in terms of both humane working conditions and of increased passenger safety. But it meant that technical advances to meet the locomotives' needs were not enough – the crew had to be considered too.

But why run non-stop? Was there any value in doing so? And how long does a railway journey between Point A and Point B have to be, to be worth describing as 'non-stop'? The first two questions are best answered in examining various non-stop services or individual runs, and the circumstances in which they were planned and made; the question of 'how long' is more easily dealt with. This book will concentrate on British railway journeys of more than 301 miles made without a *scheduled* stop of any kind, whether for passenger need or operating convenience.

And what was the longest non-stop run of all on Britain's railways? As we shall see later, it was again the human factor which entered the equation, for no railway official sanctioned or planned the longest such journey. It was the work of a crew who happened to believe its engine capable of doing the job, despite unforeseen obstacles. It is a story that sums up the best of British steam railway operation, but it is only part of a fascinating tale.

Why is non-stop railway running of particular interest to the enthusiast? The simple answers may suffice: the special arrangements made by most of the companies to ensure the collection of renewed water supplies, and (in the case of the LNER only) to change crews on long journeys without stopping, represented railway practices which are now as

Her double chimney prominent, A4 No. 60033 *Seagull*, one of the best of her class, powers effortlessly through Darlington with the up 'Capitals Limited' in July 1949. (Photomatic)

Three hundred-plus miles to go and the coal still piled high on the tender. No. 60034 *Lord Faringdon* leaving Hadley Wood South Tunnel in the late summer of 1952. (J. Davenport)

outdated as the old London and North Western or Great Western locomotives which first pushed the non-stop mileage limit towards the magic three hundred.

But there is no need for us modern rail travellers to look condescendingly on non-stop running between London and Scotland as in any way 'quaint'. No train accomplishes such a journey nowadays; not even the air companies can claim to offer city centre to city centre services without break of journey, no matter how great their advantage in speed terms. Perhaps the idea of stepping into an express train, enjoying a leisurely meal and a chance to read business documents or simply a good book, before alighting in the centre of the other capital city, is not a bad marketing concept for Inter-City to consider offering its customers while HST services still exist between London and Edinburgh (or for that matter Glasgow).

There is no technical reason to prevent such a re-introduction at the time of writing. Indeed, one of the strongest arguments against the practice of non-stop running – the lack of intermediate traffic generated – is partly nullified by the addition of passengers travelling to and from points north of Edinburgh, in the case of the present-day 'Flying Scotsman'.

Another, possibly more fanciful, reason for looking back on such trains as the 'Flying Scotsman' 'Capitals Limited', and 'Elizabethan' with such sentiment, lies in their almost

A number of the A4s were re-named after senior officers of the old LNER company. No. 60004 *William Whitelaw*, formerly *Great Snipe*, passes Brookmans Park with the up 'Elizabethan' on 4 August 1953. (Philip Kelley)

Although pictured at Greenwood in its stopping guise in October 1932, this shot of the down 'Flying Scotsman' headed by its namesake A1 No. 4472 *Flying Scotsman* was too good to exclude from this book. (Photomatic)

challenge, something which Nigel Gresley, Chief Mechanical Engineer of the LNER, could never resist. Judging by the enthusiastic way in which running- and repair-staff at certain selected depots worked on non-stop rosters, he was not alone in his eagerness to pick up any gauntlet dropped by the LNER's publicity-minded directors.

The usual stopping-places for ECML trains included Peterborough, (connecting with East Anglia and the East Midlands), Grantham (Lincoln, Nottingham, Skegness), Retford (Sheffield, Lincolnshire), Doncaster (South Yorkshire, Cleethorpes, Humberside), Selby (Hull), York (West Riding and Scarborough), Darlington (North and West ridings, Teeside) and Newcastle Upon Tyne (the largest conurbation on the route, not forgetting the curious omission of nearby Gateshead, the largest town on the line between London and Newcastle). Any train intentionally ignoring traffic to and from these important areas was inevitably something of a commercial gamble.

Critics of the LNER's non-stop ambitions have commented on the sight of lengthy rakes of heavy vehicles conveying comparatively few passengers at well below full capacity in the early- and late-summer days of the non-stop 'Flying Scotsman'. Against this, must be set the occasions mentioned by contemporary railway writers of trains running packed, with passengers standing. Certainly, what was unarguable in the between-the-wars period was the great increase in tare train weights, and this will be examined again later.

Non-Stop instead of Ever-Faster

By 1927 there was a noticeable growth of interest in running considerable distances non-stop. Radio, the cinema and illustrative journalism were making the public more conscious of the workings of the railways, and, with its stud of powerful locomotives running on a fairly easily-graded main line, the LNER began to glimpse publicity value worth extracting from its express operations.

Hampered by the anachronistic speed restriction of $8\frac{1}{4}$ hours on London–Edinburgh/ Glasgow journeys, negotiated by East and West Coast companies in October 1896 to prevent racing as in 1888 and 1895, the company aimed at the concept of long-distance, non-stop travel as a fitting publicity target. It would surely have been easier to re-negotiate the 1896 agreement, which was after all nothing more than an informal exchange of working timetables and had been openly flouted by the North Eastern Railway only five years after its signing, than to go to the trouble of making complex technical innovations to permit crew-changing at speed. Not only that, but the travelling public's interests would probably have been better served by an immediate acceleration of East Coast expresses, with the 'non-stop' principle being incorporated if so desired. (In fact, there appears to have been a thirty-minute tightening of agreed schedules on Anglo-Scottish traffic in 1923, but this proved to be ephemeral.) Needless to say, when the long-awaited speed-up was finally announced in 1932, the locomotives used were precisely those available in August 1928.

Apart from the dubious morality of continuing the 1896 agreement well beyond the period when there was an urgent need for it – in effect, forming a cartel against the public interest – the agreement was also commercially damaging. With trains taking, say, $1-1\frac{1}{2}$ hours longer than they needed to on Anglo–Scottish journeys, encouragement was being offered to their new enemy, the long-distance road coach. Although taking fifteen hours or more for the London–Edinburgh journey by 1930 (one bus operator pointedly did not even advertise any time of arrival!), road transport could be seen in a reasonably favourable light by the travelling public when the considerably lower fare was taken into account.

Ideally, a long-distance express should travel as fast as possible between its starting-point and destination, stopping at as many intermediate points as possible on the way. Illogical, unremunerative, expensive, wasteful of resources – non-stop travel between London and Scotland may have been all these things. But it was also a technical

1

Although this book is necessarily restricted to considering non-stop runs of more than 301 miles duration from 1928 to 1968, earlier moves to eliminate intermediate stops from long-distance journeys should not be forgotten.

In 1873 the longest distance run non-stop in Britain (see Appendix on p. 114) was between King's Cross and Grantham on the East Coast main line. This 105-mile distance was soon to be bettered – in the 1895 Railway Race to the North, Euston–Crewe, Crewe–Carlisle, Carlisle–Stirling on the West Coast, and Newcastle–Edinburgh on the East, comfortably exceeded this total, admittedly under exceptional conditions. But a permanent increase took place the following year when the Great Western entered the long-distance stakes.

From 1896 the Newquay portion of the 'Cornishman' express, routed via the Bristol relief line, was scheduled to travel Paddington–Exeter, 193⅝, miles, in 3¾ hours. Originally a summer service only, this working was undertaken all year round from 1899. The London and North Western capped this with the addition of over 100 miles, by running a special return working between Euston and Carlisle (299 miles each way) on 19/22 June 1903. Delegates attending the International Telegraph Conference were transported to and from the Border city in a special express grossing 450 tons and hauled by two 'Alfred' 4–4–0s on a six-hour schedule.

However, this was very much a 'one-off' event – as later West Coast non-stop achievements could similarly be categorized – and the GWR quietly set about increasing its regular long-distance mileage the following year with the timetabling of the 'Cornish Riviera Express' non-stop between Paddington and Plymouth (North Road), a distance of 245¾. miles. Two years later this impressive statistic was lessened by 20 miles with the opening of the Westbury and Castle Cary 'short-cut'. Nevertheless, for the next twenty years the Great Western Railway was second to none in its operation of long-distance, non-stopping expresses.

One fascinating 'might-have-been' could have been added to this list. In 1890, an individual named Alfred Bennett was organizing a Locomotive Annexe to an international exhibition in Edinburgh to commemorate the opening of the Forth Bridge. This involved him in touring the nation's great railway workshops personally requesting interesting, and preferably new, locomotives for display. At Crewe, none other than Francis Webb offered Bennett the latest Compound locomotive, as yet un-named, but soon to be named *Jeanie Deans*. Intriguingly, Webb offered to run the locomotive to Edinburgh non-stop from London with a press train. Bennett claimed he was told the train would arrive 'from Euston straight into the exhibition grounds without a single stop, and there pull up in front of the grand stand if we chose to provide one'.

When asked how the locomotive would fare for water north of the border, where the LNWR's ally, the Caledonian, had no water troughs, Webb assured his astonished listener that a second tender would be attached. So, what might have been the first-ever non-stop run between London and Edinburgh would have been accomplished in much the same manner as the last, seventy-eight years later. Indeed, the idea of a long-distance, non-stop train making its first stop as part of a specially-prepared exhibition was also to find an echo in the future, although on that occasion it would be a diesel locomotive receiving the acclaim. What a pity that the 1890 run was not practical, probably due to inter-company relations. In the end, *Jeanie Deans* made the journey north as part of a freight train, stopping as required.

patriotic appeal. Here you had trains crossing an international border without stopping, travelling between capital cities without the hindrance of passports and customs. Bear in mind that such running began in 1928, long before the EEC and the concept of 'Trans-Europe Express', and that the idea of England and Scotland as separate and distinct nations is one dear to many citizens, in nostalgic if not in overtly political terms.

But this is probably to over-philosophize what was basically an outstanding engineering achievement. To run a reciprocating steam locomotive *non-stop* for over eight hours on a journey of nearly four hundred miles placed a considerable burden on engine crews and maintenance men, demanding a high degree of performance from all. Not only that – but this achievement was a *daily* one. In the words of P.N. Townend, who was involved in running the 'Non-Stop' from the London end, such operations represented 'a record that has never been equalled since by any other railway in the world on a regular basis'.

Watching an IC125 achieve a recent thirty-minute turn-round at Edinburgh Waverley with all the soulless efficiency of a 'Shuttle' aircraft, one can't help feeling that 'achievement' is not part of the equation any longer. The Realist may ask, 'Why should a London–Edinburgh journey have to be an achievement, for goodness sake?', and the Romantic has no reply.

After all, the only answer is that train journeys used to excite the imagination; the 'Non-Stop' most of all.

Resplendent in Brunswick green, No. 60022 *Mallard* prepares to move off on her last non-stop trip to Edinburgh, on 2 June 1962. Nowadays this double record holder (fastest speed and longest non-stop journey for steam traction) is preserved in LNER blue with her valances restored over the driving wheels. (D.A. Anderson)

On 11 July 1927 non-stop services began between King's Cross and Newcastle, creating what was claimed as a new world record of 268¼ miles. The service concerned was the 09.50 relief to the 'Flying Scotsman', on a 5½-hour schedule every day except Tuesdays, Wednesdays and Sundays, and in the down direction only. The inaugural runs produced a hint of the excitement that was to come the following year, but there was plenty of noisy acclamation for No. 4475 *Flying Fox*, heading the first down train with Driver Pibworth at the controls (according to the RCTS definitive history of LNER locomotives; the contemporary *LNER Magazine* recording Driver Blades and Fireman Morris of Gateshead as being in charge). An enthusiastic welcoming party awaited the train's punctual arrival at Platform 8 at Newcastle Central, the crew being presented by the Lord Mayor with briar pipes donated by the railway company.

By the autumn of that year the rival LMS also grasped the publicity value of non-stop running, and, lacking the proven qualities of the Gresley Pacifics, realized the potential of competing long-distance with the LNER on equal terms – or better. After all, the lines from Euston to Glasgow (Central) and Edinburgh (Princes Street) were some nine and eight miles longer respectively than that of King's Cross to Waverley. No train could apparently complete the journey without changing crews, but the potential for record-making was there nevertheless.

With the new 'Royal Scot' locomotives expected imminently, the LMS felt confident enough about programming the 'Royal Scot' express to run non-stop over the 236 miles between Euston and Carnforth in the summer of 1927. The LNER capped this with its Newcastle dash, so its West Coast rival decided to go one better by running its 10.00 ex-Euston as far as Carlisle non-stop – a distance only a decimal point short of 300 miles. In later years this was extended over the '300' limit by stopping the train for crew-changing at Kingmoor sheds, north of the Citadel station, while maintaining the fiction of a non-stop in the public timetable. This was of course beaten in turn by the LNER, but it should be remembered that the LMS's non-stop runs over this distance were not solely confined to the summer timetable.

To travel non-stop between the capital of the British Empire and that of Scotland, four preconditions were necessary – suitable locomotives, willing crews, a means of changing them in mid-journey and water-troughs to ensure adequate fuel provision. Let us examine all four of these distinct elements in turn, in so doing gaining an insight into the constitution of what was, after all, a brand-new company, the LNER.

In 1922, with the Grouping of Britain's railways only months away, both the Great Northern and North Eastern railways produced Pacific (4–6–2) steam locomotives to haul their heaviest and fastest passenger trains. The GNR's Nigel Gresley introduced No. 1470 *Great Northern* into traffic as his first express passenger design built from scratch, although he had undoubtedly been influenced by the Pennsylvania's K4 Pacific of 1915, and had been prevented from introducing his own version by the constraints of war.

Sir Vincent Raven's 'City' Pacifics for the NER were, on the other hand, a 'stretched', but less successful, version of that designer's excellent Atlantics. Designated A2 by the LNER, they never attained the eminence of their Gresley rivals. Indeed, the last of them was withdrawn by 1937, and although they powered the 'Flying Scotsman' from time to time, they took no part in non-stop workings, and will not be considered further in this account.

Gresley's Pacific version was to be the bloodstock for East Coast motive-power until the end of steam in the 1960s. Designating the new Pacifics as A1, the LNER followed up the original twelve (LNER 4470–81) with orders for an additional forty in 1924/5. Twenty each of these were built at Doncaster (2543–62) and at the North British Locomotive works in Glasgow (2563–82).

Firmly establishing themselves as one of the most outstanding express locomotive designs in British history, the A1s suffered a slight setback in the LNER–GWR Exchange Trial of 1925, whereby a 'Castle' class 4–6–0 from the latter railway showed the Pacifics a clean pair of heels on the LNER main line out of King's Cross, while the A1 chosen for working out of Paddington made less of an impression. Some complacency seems detectable in the LNER's approach to the trial, which in any event appears to have been run without the crews being given definable remits as to coal consumption. Nevertheless, Gresley did not allow himself any excuse in reviewing the results of the Exchange, and his reaction has an important bearing on later non-stop operations.

Starting with No. 2555 *Centenary* in March 1927, the A1s were modified with long-lap travel valves, reducing coal consumption when running at speed. This improved an already impressive locomotive, but the improvement is worth quantifying. During the Exchange one unmodified A1 was found to be consuming half a hundredweight of coal per mile travelled. If non-stop journeys of nearly 400 miles were to be contemplated, then a tender accommodating ten tons of coal would be required. The original A1s had eight-wheel tenders holding eight tons of coal and 5,000 gallons of water; some improvement in this capacity would obviously have to be provided.

In fact, it was the introduction of the long-lap valve re-arrangement, bringing about a welcome drop in fuel consumption, which was the seminal event in the 'Non-Stop' story. Although after 1928, with the introduction of the corridor tender (of which more later), the A1s had the increased coal capacity to enable them to run between London and Edinburgh non-stop, the mechanical refinement demonstrated by the rival 'Castle' locomotive may *alone* have been sufficient for the A1 to undertake 400 mile non-stop running, even with the original coal capacity provided.

One Pacific, No. 4473 *Solario*, ran all the way through from Edinburgh to London on the 'Coronation' in 1938 with an original GNR tender holding eight tons of coal (while making the train's usual stop for crew and passenger purposes). This was evidence of the improved coal consumption figures produced by the long-travel valve arrangements, 34–36 lb of coal per mile being recorded by the first A1s on the regular 'Non-Stops'. (Possibly *Solario*'s achievement also owed something to Haymarket depot's ability to pack a tender with coal well above the official limit but within the loading gauge.)

Nevertheless, the LNER could hardly anticipate *Solario*'s feat of 1938 ten years earlier, nor could this reasonably be regarded as an everyday achievement allowing safe reserves of coal. After all, a tender tank run dry could be replenished at any sizeable wayside station with a water-column; a Pacific's tender run short of coal towards the end of a long-distance journey against a persistent headwind would effectively 'fail' the locomotive. A larger tender was called for as 1928 dawned. What is surprising, as we shall see later, is that this need was met while also accommodating provision for crew changing.

It is not precisely clear how the concept of the corridor tender was conceived, so the anecdote first recorded by George Dow, of the CME's daughter finding him squeezing

The fourth Gresley Pacific to be built, A1 No. 4473 *Solario* has no place in the 'official' 'Non-Stop' story on the ECML, being fitted with a GNR non-corridor tender. Yet despite this, *Solario* was able to travel throughout between Edinburgh and London on the up 'Coronation' in 1938, showing that her long-travel valves were sufficient to reduce coal consumption to a level making 393-mile journeys possible. (Photomatic)

between the back of some armchairs and the dining-room wall, seems as credible an account as any of its origin. It certainly suggests that the idea was indeed Gresley's, although it does not appear to be listed in the files of British patents.

Gresley seems to have applied for a patent on 16 May 1928 for an unspecified idea to do with locomotives, the application being abandoned before completion. From an American source mentioned below, it appears that this was in fact an application to patent the corridor tender concept, but a search undertaken by professional patents librarians on behalf of the author has failed to unearth any UK patent for a corridor tender registered in the name of Gresley, the LNER or anyone else at all. Indeed, the secrecy which cloaked the construction of these vehicles at Doncaster would surely have been unnecessary had they been patented. It may be that either the concept of a corridor through a running rail vehicle was not sufficiently innovative enough to warrant patent protection – or, most improbably, that someone had patented it already in the United Kingdom.

There is however evidence that Gresley received a patent for the idea in the United States on 15 October 1929; this is rather ironic, since, according to P.N. Townend, the Union Pacific Railroad in the USA had in 1907 designed some kind of tender connection between locomotive footplate and train for communication during testing. One wonders if such provision was pressingly necessary, as the wider and more generous loading gauge on almost any railway system except Britain's would make crew exchanges possible by means of an external walkway, if required, though admittedly without the same

L. AND N.E. RAILWAY—CORRIDOR TENDER

MR. H. N. GRESLEY, M.INST.C.E., LONDON, ENGINEER

(*For description see opposite page*)

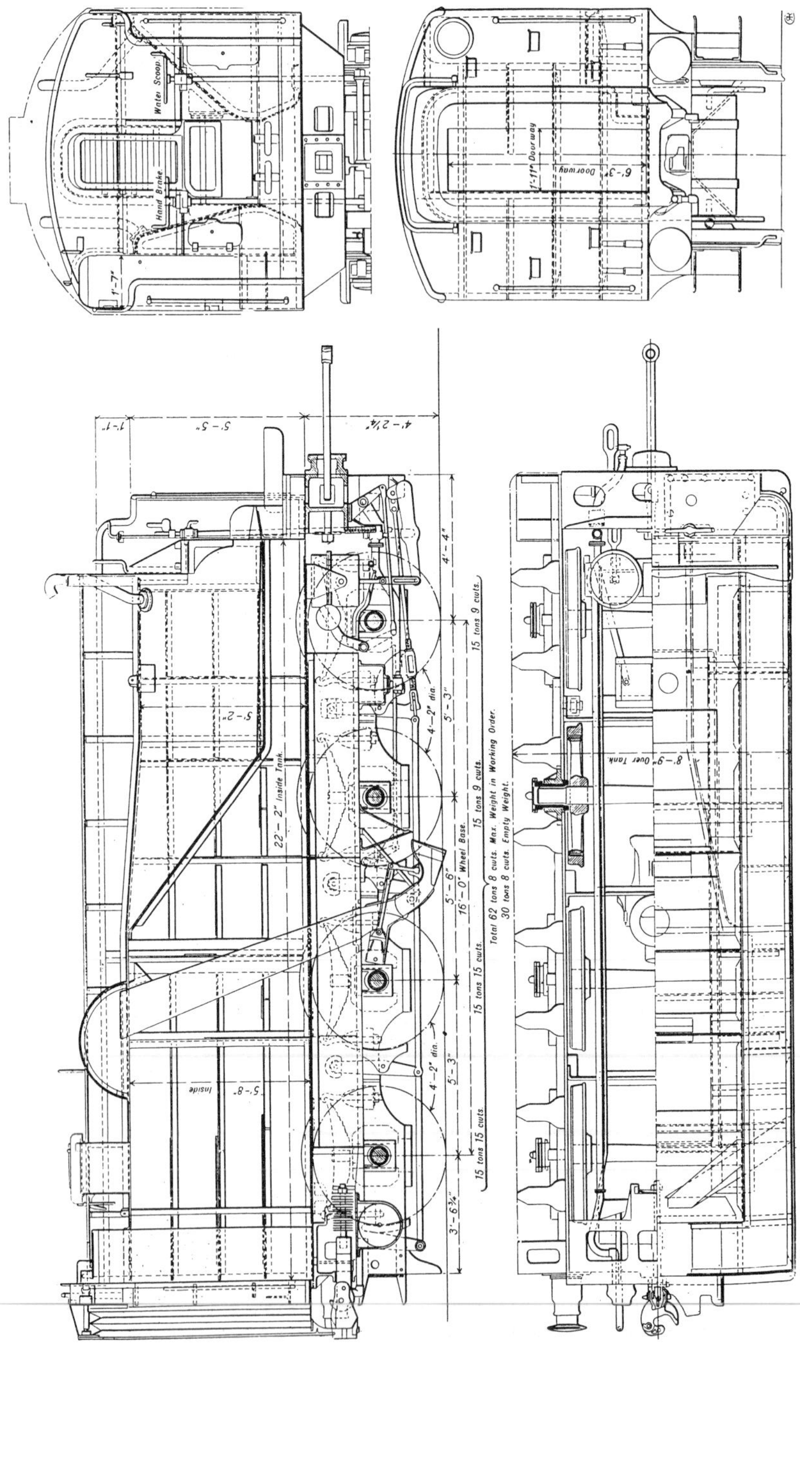

Water Scoop

Hand Brake

1'-7"

1'-1" Doorway

5'-3" Doorway

1'-6"

5'-5"

4'-2¾"

4'-4"

15 tons 9 cwts

4'-2" dia.

5'-3"

4'-2" dia.

22'-2" Inside Tank

15 tons 9 cwts

5'-6"

16'-0" Wheel Base

Total 62 tons 8 cwts. Max. Weight in Working Order.

30 tons 8 cwts Empty Weight.

15 tons 15 cwts

15 tons 15 cwts

5'-3"

4'-2" dia.

Inside

5'-8"

15 tons 15 cwts

3'-6¾"

8'-9" Over Tank

conditions of safety afforded by an internal communication. But in truth, the concept of a corridor through a tender seems obvious in retrospect, and, as for the patents mystery, the author assumes, in the absence of evidence to the contrary, that the 1928 corridor tender was not patented in the United Kingdom.

Of course, all good ideas are simple. More specifically, a corridor tender would be impossible on most other British lines simply because their tenders were so small in comparison with the LNER's. Look at the diminutive Hornby-like object hung on the back of the original LMS 'Royal Scot' 4–6–0! When one of the class ran its epic non-stop dash to Glasgow later in 1928, its tender was little larger than that attached to the 1902-vintage Midland Compound making the corresponding run to Edinburgh, although both tenders were necessarily equipped with additional coal-rails. Neither had an 18-in wide corridor running through the coals, unlike the unique innovation of the LNER.

Around the end of January 1928, the Works Manager at Doncaster was dismayed to receive an urgent order to build ten eight-wheeled corridor tenders to permit non-stop running between London and Edinburgh in the following summer, tenders which would actually increase the coal carried from eight to nine tons, without any loss of water-carrying capacity.

F.H. Eggleshaw MBE was alarmed at the very tight timetable imposed on his department in producing these unique vehicles, required for the introduction of non-stop services across the Anglo–Scottish border by 1 May. In fact, he need not have worried. Doncaster men, with their long legacy of engineering experience, did not let him down, the first tender being complete by the end of March, built in fifty working days from the receipt of the detailed design. Interestingly, the LNER's Joint Locomotive and Traffic Committee, which drew up the locomotive construction programme for 1928, did so the previous July, with no mention of any such tenders, although ten Pacifics were planned. Possibly, their ordering went into the accounts ledgers as being tenders for the 1928 Pacifics, despite the fact that they pre-dated the engines themselves, six of them being attached to existing Pacifics from the start. Given the secrecy in which they were built, more details would be welcome about the provenance of these vehicles.

Not only did the new tenders maintain the existing (very impressive) water-capacity level of 5,000 gallons, but an extra ton of coal was accommodated. This was achieved in two ways. The tender sides were built up as far as the loading gauge would allow, with coal rails reduced to a single rail half way along the offside, while the outside footplate, or 'running boards' (9 in wide on each side) were eliminated by incorporating flush sidesheets.

Most important of all, this permitted the housing of a passageway through the right-hand side of the tender, 18 in wide and 5 ft high. It emerged on the right-hand side of the cab, the train end taking a slight turn to a vestibule connection compatible with the usual train gangways. A porthole illuminated the passage from the rear end. The *Railway Gazette* reported that the tender was specially ballasted on the right hand side to compensate for the lack of coal space.

The construction of ten tenders would seem to be twice as many as required for the operation of only one long-distance service in each direction. So it comes as no surprise to learn that two other trains – the 22.50 ex-Edinburgh and 23.10 out of King's Cross – were planned for non-stop running, though this plan was not proceeded with. Overnight non-stop running might be difficult to carry out, with so many freight traffic movements at night, and with only limited publicity value resulting.

And what of the men who would traverse the corridor passage alongside the coal and the thousands of gallons of water when crossing the Plain of York? In 1919 the footplatemen's union, ASLEF, had succeeded in having an eight-hour day agreed upon by railway managements, and a standardization of footplate conditions nationally. Obviously, the 8¼-hour schedule of the 'Flying Scotsman' required two sets of crew, each working longer than half of the journey time when engine preparation and disposal is taken into account. These men were of course the 'top link' of their respective sheds, and would be required to lodge at a company hostel when on the 'away' leg of a two day trip. Interestingly, one writer close to the LNER's 'grass roots' mentions that many loco crewmen were quite prepared to work throughout between London and Edinburgh, union agreement or not. It was to the credit of the LNER that it did not give serious consideration to the idea, with all its potential for unacceptably strenuous working conditions, to say nothing of safety considerations.

What seems strange in retrospect, given that London and Edinburgh were the starting and finishing points for the famous express, was that King's Cross and Gateshead (Newcastle) depots were initially selected to operate the new non-stop service. There were two reasons for the latter shed being preferred to Haymarket (Edinburgh), despite that depot's recent acquisition of Pacifics. To begin with, the 268-mile King's Cross–Newcastle dash in 1927 was operated jointly by men from the King's Cross and Gateshead sheds; they were the men with the necessary experience of the train and the road. Indeed, Haymarket crews had not been used to working much south of Berwick, never mind Newcastle, until 1923, unless they were former NER employees based in Edinburgh.

This highlights the second reason for the LNER not initially considering Haymarket men for the 'Non-Stop'. That depot had effectively been a sub-shed of Gateshead as far as operating trains south of Edinburgh was concerned, the old North British Railway sacrificing to the North Eastern Railway the right to operate East Coast expresses between Edinburgh and Berwick in return for the dubious privilege of running powers into Newcastle from Hexham. Did the NBR really imagine that operating trains from Edinburgh down the Waverley Route to Riccarton Junction, in the wilds of the Cheviot hills, and thence over the remote Border Counties Railway to Hexham and the NER Carlisle–Newcastle line, represented a serious rival route to the East Coast main line?

Apparently it was Chief General Manager Ralph Wedgwood who suggested that Haymarket men might be rostered into the crewing arrangements for the 'Scotsman' in 1928. This had the effect of symbolically sharing the prestigious 'Scotsman' duty among men from the three LNER areas – Southern, North Eastern and Scottish – a diplomatic decision indicating the importance of the matter. A number of the Haymarket 'Top Link' were former NER men anyway (two of the four Edinburgh-based drivers first allocated to the new duty certainly were), but a fair amount of route re-familiarization was obviously necessary. Also taken at this time was the, on the face of it, strange decision to transfer for the new operation three NE-based A1s to Haymarket, which had five A1s of its own, at least three of them being converted to long-travel valves by May 1928. Gresley's assistant A.C. Stamer selected two engines from Gateshead (Nos. 2569/73) and No. 2580 from Heaton to operate from Haymarket – possibly because the latter two engines had 220 psi boilers – although this left these depots short of Westinghouse-braked units.

Not long after the start of the service, Scottish-based locomotives began working non-stop between the two British capitals, casting some doubt on the need for the transfer almost as soon as it was made. North Eastern historian Ken Hoole records that on 7 May 1928 Nigel Gresley himself agreed that the NE Area had been left without sufficient Pacific power and decided that Nos. 2569 and 2573 could be replaced on the 'Scotsman' by Haymarket's own Nos. 2563/4. This decision turned out to have a hidden complication, the English-based engines now swapping their corridor tenders for those of the Scottish engines, which were vacuum-braked instead of having the Westinghouse brake necessary for Tyneside engines. Considerable inconvenience was thus caused to the Tyneside depots by this totally unnecessary transfer. No. 2580, unlike her two NE-based sisters, spent the whole summer operating out of Edinburgh, the last time any but King's Cross or Haymarket engines were regularly allocated to the 'Non-Stop'.

Crews from Gateshead depot, however, continued to work on the service until the outbreak of the Second World War, their roster involving no fewer than three nights away from home. Before taking up their 10.00 duty out of Waverley, the NE men would work up to the Scottish capital the previous day, lodge there overnight and at King's Cross the next, after working the northern section of the up 'Non-Stop'. They would then crew the next down 'Scotsman' into Edinburgh before lodging yet again, working home to their families on the fourth day. In the circumstances it is a surprise that such an arrangement lasted as long as it did.

Ken Hoole records that the 'Non-Stop' crews were paid on a mileage basis of 200 miles for the half-journey, along with an *ex gratia* payment of one day's pay. This may seem generous for the time, meaning that Gateshead drivers on the duty were paid more than £27 a fortnight, the firemen receiving £21 over the same period. Additionally, there was a fortnightly lodging allowance of £3 15s. 11d. (roughly £3.80). These figures would have to be multiplied by a factor of about twenty-four to give a modern equivalent. If the result seems reasonable, bear in mind that each crewman coming off the first half of the journey could hardly go straight home to his wife and family. Similarly, there was the little matter for those on the second 'half' having to turn up for work four hours early. At least a meal was supplied on the train for both crews. Working the 'Non-Stop' meant a night in lodgings for at least one of the two crews; when Gateshead men were rostered, they would be lodging whether working north or south. That this arrangement lasted for no less than eleven years must have something to do with pride in the job, of being rostered for what was justifiably regarded as the most famous train in the world.

For the record, the crewmen who initiated that first summer of non-stop working were as follows; notice North Eastern men were in the majority, while two of the Haymarket men, Messrs Roper and Smith, were former NER employees:

ENGINEMEN ALLOCATED TO NON-STOP WORKINGS, MAY–SEPTEMBER 1928

Drivers	*Firemen*
Gateshead	
T. Blades	W. Morris
H. Pennington	J. Ridley
J. Gascoigne	J.J. Williams
J.W. Halford	J.F. Cairn
J.G. Smith	J. Bambra
J.G. Eltringham	J. Slinger

Haymarket

T. Henderson	R. McKenzie
T. Roper	J. Todd
R. Shedden	L. Taylor
T. Smith	J. Redpath

King's Cross

A. Pibworth	W.T. Goddard
B. Glasgow	A. Austin
J. Day	F. Gray
H. Miles	W.J. Bridle

With 13,000 gallons of water expected to be consumed by the locomotive on an average non-stop journey, the provision of water-troughs was obviously a crucial consideration. These were located at strategic intervals on the East Coast main line at locations indicated on the accompanying plan. The first for northbound trains was at Langley, just south of Stevenage; its location only twenty-seven miles out from King's Cross suggests it was more heavily used by up trains, since a Gresley Pacific tender was quite capable of sustaining an express over 125 miles or more.

Fifty-two miles farther north lay Werrington troughs, located before trains began the gradual but demanding climb of Stoke Bank. Muskham troughs were situated near Retford and were an identical length (704 yards) to those at Scrooby (sometimes known as Bawtry), some nine miles south of Doncaster. From here on, there were only two sets of troughs laid by the old North Eastern Railway to cover the near-250 miles on to Edinburgh – at Wiske Moor, just north of Northallerton, and at Lucker, fifteen miles south of Berwick. Wiske Moor to Lucker without stopping for water was, in the opinion of acknowledged expert Cecil J. Allen, likely to pose the most serious fuel-consumption problem of any non-stop Anglo–Scottish journey, and the need for fuel economy was one contributing factor in his oft-repeated opinion about the inferior running of LNER East Coast trains north of the former Great Northern line.

On average, each trough took approximately five minutes to refill; not an insignificant statistic given the LNER's practice of programming expresses (particularly in the down direction) into 'convoys'. This policy was intended to facilitate paths for slower traffic by concentrating the faster trains into recognizable patterns, say between 09.00 and 10.30 or 16.00 and 18.00 out of King's Cross. Obviously, the trackside pumping arrangements had to be capable of keeping the vital troughs replenished if out-of-course stops were to be avoided. Interestingly, there was a unique occasion in 1954 when two non-stop trains ran northwards over the East Coast main line after starting from King's Cross within ten minutes of each other – and the troughs failed the second train only once out of six water pick-up operations. Admirable though that may have been, it was of course sufficient to force the second train to an unscheduled halt – but that story will be told later.

At 18 in wide, steam-age water-troughs were designed to permit a train travelling at 35 mph (although in practice, at anything up to twice this speed) to pick up 2,000 gallons, dipping to a depth of 3 in. This last statistic was a crucial one; after the Grouping of 1923 the GNR and NER found that the former's wooden troughs were $7\frac{1}{4}$ in deep with water

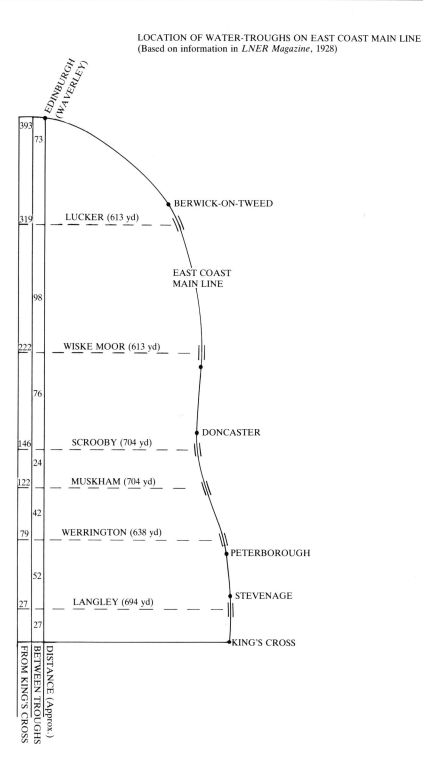

LOCATION OF WATER-TROUGHS ON EAST COAST MAIN LINE
(Based on information in *LNER Magazine*, 1928)

Nameplate of the preserved A3, No. 4472, later BR. No. 60103. (Courtney Haydon)

level 1 in above rail level, the engine's scoop going down to a depth of $2\frac{1}{2}$ in. It was decided to standardize on a uniform water level of 2 in above rail, with the scoop of a fully-laden tender entering to a depth 1 in below the rail level. Adjustments were only finalized the week before non-stop running began; it was a detail that could not be overlooked.

Gresley was reportedly worried about the water supply on the section of the run north of York, when non-stop services were initiated to Newcastle in 1927. An improved valve arrangement at Wiske Moor was installed in time for the new non-stop services, and early in 1928 it was decided to test the efficacy of water-collection over this stretch. On 10 February, No. 2568 *Sceptre* hauled a 450-ton special from York to Edinburgh, succeeding in picking up 2,387 gallons at Wiske Moor and rather more at Lucker. This gave a consumption of around 6,500 gallons at 31.5 to the mile.

This banished almost all remaining doubts about the practicality of non-stop running over 300 miles or more. More detailed studies on this matter were done in post-war years, and are discussed later, but there was no doubt that the southern half of the East Coast route was more highly favoured with water provision; indeed Wiske Moor and Lucker took on the status of oases in a northern desert. Coming southwards, it would be found that Pacifics would have less than 20 per cent water reserves as they approached Scrooby, where a maximum pick-up would be essential, to be topped up further at

Muskham, only twenty-four miles farther south. It only emphasized that daily non-stop running was certainly practicable, but there was no room for error.

One other detail was lubrication; Wakefield mechanical lubricators were becoming available with a greater capacity than the Detroit pattern then prevalent. No special lubricant appears to have been necessary for the runs to come – perhaps just a little more being necessary than before!

Pirates steal
the Blue Riband

On Tuesday 1 May 1928 the LNER intended to inaugurate its non-stop 'Flying Scotsman' service between London and Edinburgh, taking advertising space in most national dailies to announce the fact. (This was not the least of the reasons why railway matters received a reasonable amount of corresponding text column inches.) The reader of *The Times* and *Scotsman* was given every opportunity to grasp the fact that the LNER planned a major improvement in its long-distance passenger services from that date, with the introduction of the 'Queen of Scots' Pullman as well as the 'non-stop' achievement. As far as the latter was concerned the advertisement emphasised the

'corridor through tender,
fresh driver and fireman
take control whilst running'.

It was an unusually technical point to make to the general public about the operation of a train. It assumed an intelligent level of public interest, and this confidence was, as we shall see, not altogether misplaced.

In welcoming the idea of non-stop running over long distances, the *Railway Gazette* commented that the concept would be economical in locomotive provision, and advised the LNER not to be put off by an obscure American claim for a 448-mile 'stunt' journey made non-stop 'many years ago'. The LNER was not only undismayed by this claim, it simply ignored it, and it has never apparently surfaced again in British railway literature, to this author's knowledge (See Appendix on p. 114).

Everything was ready for the month of May to arrive and for the LNER to claim the blue riband of long-distance rail operation, for which it was uniquely equipped, by breaking the 301 mile 'barrier' for the first time.

Who at King's Cross was to know that there were pirates abroad?

As 1928 dawned, the LMS was the holder of the world's regular non-stop record. Throughout the 1927-8 winter the 'Royal Scot' express ran the 299 miles from Euston to Carlisle without an intermediate stop, unlike the LNER which operated its King's Cross–Newcastle run (thirty-one miles shorter) in the summer only.

Carlisle really seemed to be the limit of a northbound run for one crew. The 299 miles to Carlisle Citadel, the alternative crew-changing site being Kingmoor sheds a shade over the 300-mile mark from London, needed 5½–6 hours of constant concentration in driving

and firing, even if there had been little or no schedule improvement since the summer of 1903 when *Charles H. Mason* and *Commonwealth*, two 'Alfred' class 4-4-0s, had taken their lucky trainload of telegraphy engineers on what was then the longest non-stop run in the world. But to travel all the way from London to Edinburgh or Glasgow meant an eight-hour journey – an impossible demand for one crew. The company's own rule-book forbade more than three people on the footplate at one time, so even taking a duplicate crew was out of the question. Not only that, but the locomotives had to be efficient enough not to require more coal than their tenders could carry, and tender development had simply not kept pace with the rival on the east.

In other words, a regular non-stop service across the border was obviously out of the question. But the LNER's publicity machine had to be silenced somehow . . .

On Friday 27 April 1928, intending passengers arriving at Euston for the northbound 'Royal Scot' found the train divided into two sections, one each for Glasgow and Edinburgh. The former left normally at ten o'clock with 'Royal Scot' 4-6-0 No. 6113 *Cameronian* heading eight coaches. Five minutes later Compound 4-4-0 No. 1054 followed with a six-coach Edinburgh portion. Both locomotives had temporarily been allocated higher-sided tenders than usual.

'Traffic conditions at Euston ...necessitated the running of the train in duplicate.' This was to be the official reason (and a highly dubious one) for this unusual dual arrangement, and it is unlikely that railway enthusiasts were fooled for very long. It is more likely that word got around fairly quickly – the LMS were going to break the LNER's 393 mile record before it was even made! Despite the secrecy – which reduced the pressure to succeed on the respective crews – it was nevertheless a valiant gesture. Two express trains together running more than 800 miles without a stop, and one of the locomotives a 4-4-0 of the type introduced on the Midland Railway in 1902! Their route included fifteen miles at around 1 in 80 to reach the summits of Shap and Beattock while, in addition, No. 1054 also had to face the climb to Cobbinshaw summit east of Carstairs junction. Compared to such a mountainous route, the 'Flying Scotsman's' the following week was a veritable billiard table.

The passengers on the trains were pleasantly surprised when, passing Symington at express speed, they realised that they were participating in the making of a new record, and on alighting a number were eager to congratulate the enginemen on their achievement. (*Scotsman*)

The Lanarkshire wayside station of Symington was the usual stop for the splitting of the Glasgow and Edinburgh sections, and even alert passengers would not have suspected some strange goings-on before then, since the usual engine-change point at Carlisle was not publicized in the timetable, and the absence of such a stop on this occasion might well have gone unremarked.

Arrival at Glasgow Central was seven minutes early, the 4-4-0 reaching Edinburgh (Princes Street) at 18.08, two minutes early (presumably on the working timetable). The crewmen receiving the congratulations at Central were Driver Stones and Fireman Pink, accompanied by Driver Gibson of Polmadie, Glasgow. The last named took the regulator on the second part of the run, with each driver assisting the fireman when not at the regulator. At Edinburgh, the crew who jumped down onto the platform 'as fit as

Pirates steal the Blue Riband of non-stop running! This is believed to be the first-ever publication of a photograph of the LMS 'Royal Scot' express which set a British and European non-stop record of 401 miles between London and Glasgow on 27 April 1928, three days before the LNER started its non-stop 'Flying Scotsman'. The locomotive is 'Royal Scot' class 4–6–0 No. 6113 *Cameronian* pictured on Beattock bank with its specially lightened train. (R.B. Haddon collection, Mitchell Library)

fiddles' – as the local newspaper described them – were Driver Langdale and Fireman Bassett, 'conducted' north of the border by Driver Ballantine of Dalry Road depot, Edinburgh.

Enthusiasm at the northern termini knew no bounds, not equalled, at least in Edinburgh's case, until the following Tuesday, one newspaper describing No. 1054 looking 'as if it had just arrived from a branch-line run'. This same report solemnly assured its readers that the 4–4–0 had enough coal for a return trip. When asked if this non-stop run (a record by a round 100 miles) was to become a normal working, a LMS official said: 'The opportunity had simply been taken of demonstrating the possibilities of the very efficient locomotives of the LMS Railway.'

One railway historian has called it 'vainglorious', but it was a superb example of Anglo-Scottish railwaymen's co-operation in response to a challenge from a superior rival. The newspapers were too polite to ask how the crews answered calls of nature, or even how they ate meals, during the 8¼-hour runs. The LMS in fact had made no arrangements whatsoever for such straightforward human requirements; it was simply happy to harness the railwayman's genuine love of the job. Similarly, LNER men had been, as we have seen, trying to persuade their officials to allow them to work throughout on the East Coast main line without proper relief provisions. Gresley's corridor tender employed sanity and humanity to solve the problem.

1928: The Year of the Non-Stop

Tuesday 1 May 1928 saw the LNER prepare for the start of non-stop operations as if the LMS record was nothing more than a bad dream. In a sense, the events of the previous Friday had taken on a fairly ephemeral aspect anyway, with no attempt by the LMS to introduce regular non-stop running. Besides, the LNER's intended operations were undoubtedly a more formidable undertaking.

Carrying out a record run without previous announcement, as *Cameronian*, No. 1054, and their crews had achieved, did not involve the same onus to succeed as a loudly trumpeted press build-up to a record attempt. The 'fourth estate' loves nothing more than to report the pride that comes before a fall, with any such hubris being guaranteed maximum publicity.

The LNER was on a hiding to nothing. If it succeeded, no record had been broken; if it failed, everyone would know.

For the first northbound run, King's Cross selected the most appropriate locomotive possible – No. 4472 *Flying Scotsman* itself. She would be crewed by Driver Pibworth and Fireman Goddard on the southern section of the run, with Messrs Blades and Morris of Gateshead taking over north of York. Inspector Bramall was assigned to accompany the crews. In fact, an even more distinguished footplate visitor, none other than Nigel Gresley himself, was to feature among those who would make their way from the passenger accommodation to the engine cab during the journey.

Haymarket chose one of the North Eastern-based Pacifics so recently received on transfer – No. 2580 *Shotover*. Her crews would comprise locally-based Driver Henderson and Fireman McKenzie, with Driver Day and Fireman Gray of King's Cross travelling 'on the cushions' for the first half of the trip. Inspector Renton accompanied them, later contributing a valuable record of the up journey to the *LNER Magazine*.

The coaching stock was recorded in the following configuration (from the engine): brake van with three Third class compartments (the first of these reserved for the resting crews), a Third class, First and Third class, Third class restaurant car, kitchen car, First class restaurant car, First class, hairdressing saloon and ladies' resting room (with five Third class compartments), two more Third class, and brake van. Notice that there was no nonsense about First and Third class passengers eating in the same coach!

The stock had been specially constructed for the service in 1924 but contained no outstanding interior decor, in comparison with catering vehicles due to be introduced

A unique picture of the first ever non-stop run between Edinburgh and London. On 1 May 1928, A3 No. 2580 *Shotover* was photographed at speed passing Croft Spa with the up 'Flying Scotsman'. *Shotover* was normally based at the former NER depot of Heaton (Newcastle), and her Westinghouse brake pump is visible on the running-board. (Photomatic)

later that summer. More interesting was the conversion of an ordinary vehicle into a hairdressing saloon and made available equally to First and Third class passengers. The technical press at the time conveyed the LNER's solemn assurances about the smooth running of its coaching stock on track of unapproachable excellence. This was presumably to pre-empt any press speculation about slipping scissors!

Surrounded by pressmen and fascinated members of the public on that memorable Tuesday, London's Lord Mayor, Sir Charles Batho, inspected the locomotive and spoke of British railways leading the world. Meanwhile, at Waverley, a similar scene was unfolding as ten o'clock neared. Bailie Hay, deputizing for the indisposed Lord Provost, Sir Alexander Stevenson, was accompanied by his daughter who pinned black and white rosettes on the enginemen's lapels and supplied a similarly-beribboned horsehoe for the locomotive itself.

Also coloured black and white – and this was much more historic from a railway point of view – was a 'Flying Scotsman' headboard painted black on white, supplied by Haymarket depot to crown *Shotover*'s smokebox. The style was very much that of the NBR destination-type headboard, although with a reversal of colours, and was probably the first of its kind to be seen at King's Cross – though not the last. 'Top Shed's' tinsmiths apparently got busy in fashioning their own version of the unofficial board, the general design of which, as we know, was to become standard equipment for British express trains in the age of steam and beyond.

Ten o'clock arrived and the up and down versions of the LNER's most important train pulled out simultaneously on that far-off May Day. The company had invited the press to

attend and report; now the railwaymen had to travel farther than any train had ever been advertised to do. Failure would be ignominious. *Flying Scotsman*, *Shotover*, and their crews and maintenance men had two trains to deliver over a combined distance of nearly 800 miles – and on time.

But not only were eight crewmen under the microscope. Two hundred signalmen had to pull over eight hundred levers in the space of the next eight hours on the East Coast main line. Control staff had to be sure that the paths were clear, that no stopping passenger or goods train was occupying the vital section when the 'Scotsman' required to enter it. The whole LNER system was on trial.

With both trains well and truly 'launched' by the civic leaders of both capital cities, it is opportune, before following their progress, to cast a critical eye over this now vanished mode of transport, so far removed from the utilitarian IC125s monopolizing the East Coast mainline at the present time.

A 'crawling caravanserai' was how Gresley's biographer F.A.S. Brown was later to describe the 48 mph 'Flying Scotsman' of 1928, and the railway historian can only be baffled by the slow scheduled pace. This was slightly faster south of Grantham, 52 mph being required to be maintained to keep the 'Scotsman' out of the path of its own relief (10.05 out of King's Cross) but, north of York, 45 mph was the average speed of this crack express. Geoffrey Hughes has pointed out that dead fish landed at Aberdeen could reach London faster than passengers travelling on the East Coast in the thirty-five years up to 1932! Even the contemporary newspapers were soon to scent a whiff of such a scandalous state of affairs.

While the events of 1 May were given maximum publicity, no newspaper mentioned the unsatisfactory speed of the train in their reports of that day. But only seventy-two hours later *The Times* published a letter from a Mr Kitto of Glasgow comparing the 'Scotsman's' speed unfavourably with that of the Great Western's 'Cornish Riviera Express', itself no mean achiever in the non-stop stakes. In commenting on the undoubted speed potential of the Gresley Pacifics and 'Royal Scots', he asked, 'Will not the LMS and LNER now consent to allow their nice new engines to enjoy themselves?'

On the same day one of the Scottish newspapers published a report, originating for no known reason in Carlisle, that there was a 'speed control arrangement' between the two rival companies designed to keep the timing above eight hours. This was of course absolutely correct but neither railway commented and the matter was not pursued. Indeed, the newspapers, far from asking pertinent questions about a cartel blighting the speed of Anglo–Scottish train services, were bent on recording such vital facts as the number of haircuts and shaves administered to passengers during the non-stop journeys! (Eighteen and three respectively on the first up journey; the numbers for the down trip are not known. The author will no doubt be forgiven for not troubling to research this point further!)

Only a year later, LNER Pacific No. 2750 *Papyrus*, later to be immortalized in a semi-fictional book (see Bibliography), showed what a nonsense the 'Scotsman's' timetable was. With Driver Gutteridge at the controls, *Papyrus* chopped twenty-seven minutes off what the newspapers were assuring everyone was the crack schedule of the up 'Flying Scotsman', in an effort to make up time lost earlier on the run. This achievement, on 23 May 1929, was not carried out on a non-stop schedule – which was theoretically even easier – the summer starting-date for such 1929 operations being later in the year than in 1928.

No. 2580 *Shotover* on the first 'up' run of the new 'Flying Scotsman', 1 May 1928, seen shortly after arrival at King's Cross. The two locomotive crews are being congratulated by the Chairman of the LNER, William Whitelaw – forebear of the present Lord Whitelaw – who is seen handing a souvenir pocket book to each man. Notice in particular the headboard carried by the engine; this was hastily prepared for the train by the staff at Edinburgh Haymarket shed and in keeping with the type of board carried on local services in that area. The idea was then copied by King's Cross shed and was to result in the principal named trains of all four railway companies carrying headboards for the first time. (Hulton Picture Company)

But to any knowledgeable observer of the British railway scene, it must all have seemed so disappointing. C.J. Allen addressed himself to the matter in the *Railway Magazine*, estimating that the down 'Scotsman' was being granted an extra twenty-five minutes to spin out on its journey, and the up train no less than thirty-one, given that the following relief trains kept the same timing inclusive of four stops. He pointed out that the non-stop nature of this important Anglo–Scottish train prohibited it from being of any assistance to its hard-pressed relief at busy times, making the working of the latter train correspondingly more difficult and thereby possibly incurring extra costs in running a relief to the relief, as it were. Of course, he may have unconsciously touched on the justification of not stopping at intermediate stations over a record distance when he commented in another issue of the same magazine on 'the extraordinary amount of publicity given to it [the non-stop service] in the press'.

At two minutes past two on 1 May 1928, up and down 'Scotsmen' crossed at Alne, north of York. The northbound train was soon to make railway history by being the first express from the south to thread its way alongside Platform 8 in Newcastle Central without stopping, the crew no doubt having received whistles and cheers from their

mates at Gateshead. (One wonders what the staff of Heaton depot, on the north side of Newcastle, thought seeing their engine, *Shotover*, on the corresponding up train. It was in fact a locomotive from this comparatively 'unglamorous' shed which was to receive the cheers at the southern end.)

Shotover's train had reportedly had the more difficult journey up to that time, but, even so, was one minute early at York. The Haymarket crew had had to deal with heavy mist on the Scottish section of the run, although newspaper reports indicated that four minutes had been dropped between Berwick and Newcastle. All of it was recouped by York with a minute to spare, the first handing-over point obviously being seen by the northern crew as a responsibility to be handled punctually.

Inspector Renton accompanying the southbound crews, with their eleven-coach, 323 ton, tareload, seems to have thoroughly enjoyed himself, glorying in the 'lusty cheers' at the principal stations on the line, 'the locomotive centres being particularly enthusiastic'. None more so than Doncaster, where Eggleshaw noted his men, and those of the other parts of the works, taking time out of their allotted lunch-breaks to cheer the northbound 'Scotsman' through, effectively closing a bridge to road traffic, so great was their number.

Writing later in the *LNER Magazine*, Renton was quite unable to conceal his pride in the reception the train received at King's Cross. Like George Dow, he was moved by the sight of the arrival platform packed from end to end by a cheering throng, writing later:

The feat is a great compliment to Mr Gresley . . . The performance of the engine was splendid in every respect, and in the opinion of the enginemen and myself, nothing finer in the shape of a steam locomotive could be asked for. Coal consumption, including lighting-up and raising steam, [was] six tons, 34.02 lbs of coal consumed per engine-mile, and a water consumption that averaged about 2,500 gallons per 100 miles . . . [the engine was] steaming freely during the latter part of the journey. I am proud of having been associated with the enginemen on this first non-stop run on our line between Edinburgh and London.

Northbound, the crews received an unexpected bonus – a whipround of £10 from the grateful passengers, in addition to the inscribed pocket-books donated by the company to all eight footplatemen on both trains. But unknown to the passengers, the Gateshead crew were fighting a serious hazard to the train's scheduled non-stop status. A tender axle-box was running 'hot', the fireman desperately playing a cold-water hose on it as they neared the Scottish capital. This is not mentioned in the newspaper reports or the LNER's staff magazine, but is recorded in the authoritative RCTS history of the LNER's Pacifics. One lucky footplate visitor, Charles S. Lake of the *Railway Gazette*, was personally escorted to the cab by none other than Nigel Gresley himself at some stage of the Berwick–Edinburgh stretch, and the crew appear to have been working normally at that point, according to Lake's later published account. It is surely inconceivable that the crew would disguise such a crisis from their CME – after all, it could have incapacitated the engine and ruined the occasion – so the problem may only have been spotted quite near to Edinburgh. Another technical journalist, Douglas Seaton, had also been privileged to ride on the footplate in Gresley's company and went so far as to record that on arrival at Waverley 'all bearings were cool'.

Overheating or not, the express's arrival at Waverley was twelve minutes early, despite some nine minutes being lost to permanent way restrictions, implying a nett gain of twenty-one minutes to the locomotive. *Flying Scotsman* had hauled her approximate 400-ton train-load in grand style, an estimated two tons of coal remaining on the tender. Not one signal check had been encountered – the unseen battalion of two hundred signalmen had done their work well. Following attention at Haymarket depot, No. 4472 was able to work home the next day.

Perhaps the last word on the happenings of that far-off May Day could be left with Driver Henderson, driver of the up train on the first half of its journey. Interviewed among the crush at King's Cross, the Scottish engineman commented that the corridor tender arrangement had been a complete success but complained that he had been unable to have his hair cut before reaching London!

So began the first of twelve pre-war seasons of non-stop running between London and Edinburgh. On the second day (2 May), with both of the first day's featured engines, *Flying Scotsman* and *Shotover*, working home, the London arrival was five minutes early, the northbound train being no less than fifteen to the good. Douglas Seaton had returned to London on the second day's up train, and apparently enjoyed a footplate run for part of the journey. He recorded that there was only one unexpected check for No. 4472. This was at Selby North box where a distant signal failed to clear, and the home only 'fell to off' as the train braked. This caused 'consternation' on the footplate, proving that, in the early days of the 'Flying Scotsman' at least, 'non-stop' meant exactly that. On the third day, King's Cross substituted No. 2546 *Donovan* (a locomotive which appears to have been fitted with a corridor tender for only four days) for No. 4472, the latter resuming two days later.

Six weeks later, the 'Flying Scotsman' was in the news again, challenged once more in its proud role as Britain's premier means of public transport. But this time the 'challenger' was not a LMS 'Royal Scot' or Midland Compound. It was a competitor from literally out of the blue.

The Air/Rail Race to Edinburgh

In one of the most bizarre episodes ever involving an East Coast express – indeed, any British train – Class A1 Pacific No. 2563 *William Whitelaw* sprinted for Edinburgh with the non-stop 'Flying Scotsman', pursued and overtaken – by a plane!

The date was 15 June 1928, the occasion an exercise to compare the merits of rail and air transport. Although not strictly a race, the simultaneous working of a flight and non-stop rail journey between London and Edinburgh was seen as a means of direct comparison between the two modes of transport, and was made in the full glare of publicity. The media made much ado of the established (by implication slightly 'stuffy') character of the 'Flying Scotsman', with its sixty-six-year pedigree, in comparison with the elitist and exciting means of aerial transport between the capitals.

The initiative for this demonstration had come from Imperial Airways, the forerunner of the present British Airways. Imperial was anxious to raise public consciousness of air travel, hoping particularly to create a demand for local authority funding for airports or airline subsidy, as on the German model. The airline may also have been nettled by the publicity the LNER and LMS had received for their non-stop running exploits already that year, and suggested this simultaneous event to divert publicity to itself.

Imperial's flight was no less a unique undertaking than the LMS's non-stop dash to Edinburgh and Glasgow the previous April, with no immediate effort being made to introduce a domestic service in regular rivalry with the rail companies. Such airborne services did not properly begin for another six years, when, interestingly, the LNER and the other three Grouping companies partnered Imperial Airways in Railway Air Services, offering an indirect limited-capacity link between London and Glasgow via Belfast. In fact, the Glasgow engineering firm of Beardmore had attempted to inaugurate a Glasgow (Renfrew)–London (Cricklewood) service as early as the summer of 1920, using its own aircraft (with capacity for a single passenger!). However, the proving flights appear not to have been successful enough to encourage continuing, using larger aeroplanes.

If Imperial's purpose was a purely publicity-catching exercise, it succeeded admirably, as we shall see. In fact, the 1928 incident showed up the LNER in a fairly dim light – and needlessly so.

The day of the journey, 15 June 1928, began with a breakfast at London's Savoy Hotel attended by about fifty travellers. All of the airborne party were present, along with a small fraction of the three hundred passengers who had booked in advance for seats on the train. They heard that Sir Ralph Wedgwood, Chief General Manager of the LNER, would welcome them to the Scottish capital after their respective journeys, and they were wished Godspeed by a leading director of Imperial.

As the train's traditional departure time of ten o'clock neared, the two parties made their way to King's Cross and Croydon Airport respectively. Punctually at ten, the three propellors of the rather inappropriately-named *City of Glasgow* biplane, an Armstrong-Siddeley Argosy 'De Luxe', roared into life and lifted her complement of twenty-one, including the Director of Civil Aviation, Air Vice-Marshall Sir William Sefton Brancker, into the sky. Meanwhile at King's Cross, an A1 Pacific eased its massive train out of the platform.

So fascinated were the newspapers by the novelty of the London–Edinburgh flight, that comparatively few details of the train are recorded. We know from the *LNER Magazine* (not from the newspapers) that the locomotive was Haymarket-based No. 2563 *William Whitelaw*, indicating some adjustment in operating practices since the introduction of the new service, as a former Heaton engine transferred to Edinburgh had headed the early 'Non-Stops' instead of No. 2563 and her Haymarket sisters. Some newspapers gave its load as 500 tons, although the rake actually consisted of twelve coaches, grossing around 430 tons. A relief express, the 'Junior Scotsman', was due to leave only five minutes later – and it too will feature later in our story.

Already *City of Glasgow* was thrilling her select passengers with a view of the Thames

Involved in the 'race' with the Imperial Airways Argosy in June 1928, A1 No. 2563 *William Whitelaw* enters Newcastle (Central) with a down non-stop 'Flying Scotsman'. (Photomatic)

estuary as she turned northwards towards the Essex coast near Southend. For many of them this was their first trip aloft, and they were fortunate to experience flight in near-perfect conditions. One of the fliers was James Birkett, a former LNER driver of seventy-nine, whose role was to help the pilot, Captain Gordon P. Olley, identify the train which they were expected to accompany northwards. Radio links were to be maintained between air and rail, with the 'Flying Scotsman' being awarded a one-year broadcasting (receiving) licence specially for the purpose, according to press reports. It is not clear if this was the same equipment installed in the up and down trains earlier in the month by McMichael & Co., at the invitation of the LNER Information Department, so that train-bound passengers could listen in to a radio commentary of the Derby. (Incidentally, it was won by Felstead, a name which was to grace the first of the new A3s to emerge from Doncaster within two months.)

After one hour of flying in beautiful weather at round 500 ft, the aeroplane was approaching Lowestoft. According to one newspaper writer this meant that the rival train would be passing Peterborough – something hardly likely on the 'Scotsman's' dawdling 48 mph average schedule.

But the airborne travellers had no interest in this; they were enjoying what Imperial Airways pointed out was literally an East Coast route to Scotland. Obviously the coastline was a simple aviation aid for the pilot to follow but Captain Olley later told the Press Association that he had deliberately strayed across the Norfolk Broads in order to wave to relatives holidaying on a houseboat! After surveying Great Yarmouth and Cromer, touch-down was made at about 12.20 p.m. at Bircham Newton, near King's Lynn. How long was spent here by the *City of Glasgow* is unclear, the pilot later referring to a 'a 15 minute delay waiting for petrol'; presumably the overall time spent on the ground was at least twice as long as this.

There was to be no break for the 'Flying Scotsman'. Her fuel replenishment was by water-trough, a principle as old as the tradition surrounding the express itself, with its 1862 provenance. Her slow pace is puzzling to us looking back through the clouded glass of history. Did railway enthusiasts aboard not feel frustrated that such fine engines as Gresley's Pacifics were not allowed to go faster? The LNER train's non-stop character, coupled to its boast of being one of Britain's oldest named trains, seemed sufficient to prevent criticism of its dismal speed. Of course, this air-rail demonstration was not a race, although one wonders if the crews were itching to open the regulator just a little further . . . .

The newpapers assure us that the air passengers enjoyed 'Pullman' comfort on their flight, waited on by a steward, though the hospitality could hardly have matched that of the rival train. Indeed, the *Railway Gazette* went so far as to point out the futility of any such comparison on grounds of comfort, arguing that the larger the unit of transport, the more comfort it could offer its passengers. Gresley's brand-new triplet restaurant car set, with its Louis XVI décor, would not go into service for another month on the 'Flying Scotsman' express, but even so, the existing stock was only four years old. The train's cocktail bar was only a little in the future.

By mid-afternoon the train crew had been renewed, the northern footplatemen relieving their southern colleagues as the train crossed the Vale of York. Above them, the rival travellers had met more variable weather conditions. The *City of Glasgow* passed over Skegness and looked down on Hartlepool in bright sunshine, but the pilot was later to talk of storms over Yorkshire, and the earlier fine weather seems to have become scarcer as the border was neared. Indeed, one paper mentioned 'air sickness' but this point was not laboured! The plane's second stop was made at Cramlington, just north of Newcastle. Here, significantly, one journalist wrote of a welcome cup of tea being served, so perhaps catering was not quite as 'Pullman' as some of the papers would have us believe! This second break lasted from 3.45 p.m. to 4.20 p.m., with more refuelling.

The Royal Border Bridge at Berwick-on-Tweed seems to have been an important landmark on this June day, and one which raises questions about the alleged non-competitiveness which ruled the day's operations. It was apparently agreed beforehand that plane and train would 'rendezvous' at the Border Bridge before proceeding northwards. Since there was presumably no question of the train stopping, it was tacitly understood that the plane would reach the Tweed first and would await the 'Scotsman'. The press were so informed and the Sporting and General Photo-Agency despatched a photographer to cover the event.

Indeed, judging by the significance of the bridge to the Imperial crew, not to mention every single newspaper covering the event, the LNER evidently failed to mention to anyone that the real Anglo-Scottish border is some three miles north of the Royal Border Bridge. The Lamberton Toll 'frontier' site was not marked for a further nine years, when the signs 14 ft wide by some 9 ft high, were erected in the first half of 1937.

However, when the 'Flying Scotsman' reached the Tweed crossing, there was no aeroplane to be seen. Obviously, the footplate crew pressed on without stopping, no apparent radio contact being received at this point. Meanwhile, *City of Glasgow* was some three minutes behind schedule but was still in good time to circle the bridge as an express steamed below. Irritatingly however, there was no answering flashlight from the 'Scotsman's' fourth carriage – the agreed acknowledgement to the plane's radio contacts, there being no transmitter in the express. Much worse, the air passengers realized that the express was slowing to a stop at Berwick station – they were 'buzzing' the wrong train! Presumably Mr Birkett, the LNER's aged representative, was unable to advise the flight deck of their mistake in time, or perhaps he too misidentified the 'Junior Scotsman' as its non-stop predecessor. Whatever caused this error, there was now no more exhibition flying – it was off northwards, with a vengeance!

Nevertheless, the *Railway Gazette* soon published a Sporting and General photograph, taken from Berwick Castle, clearly showing No. 2563 *William Whitelaw*, replete with 'Flying Scotsman' headboard, crossing the bridge with a three-engine plane flying a couple of hundred feet above. Yet, the newspapers at the time made clear that this rendezvous did not in fact take place, and Captain Olley later confirmed this in the *LNER Magazine*. The provenance of the photograph must be adjudged obscure.

One newspaper records that the train's radio operator had heard the plane's radio messages when already over the border, but was, understandably, unable to see the plane. But no matter, the 'ten o'clock' was now hurtling down Cockburnspath bank, and the airliner did not catch up until Dunbar at about 5.25 p.m. This put the train only twenty-nine miles from Edinburgh (Waverley) and one can imagine that the Pacific was being accelerated for all she was worth from the Dunbar slack. Even so, the crew and passengers could not have been too optimistic as they saw the 115 mph-capable *City of Glasgow* cruise off westwards towards the Scottish capital.

Captain Olley was later to claim that, on resighting the express, he apologized twice for his lateness and informed the 'Scotsman' that he would have 'to push ahead to land, as the air party wished to be on the platform at Waverley to meet the train contingent *as arranged*'. Did they indeed! And had the LNER really agreed to the plane arriving first, or had such a prospect simply seemed so probable as to make agreement inevitable?

So we come to the conclusion of the eight-hour journey, when suddenly the pedantic schedule seemed not to matter any more – all that did was to get there first!

The 'Flying Scotsman' burst out of the Calton tunnel into the Waverley platforms – and found that it was the 'winner', eleven minutes early.

'The jubilation of the engine driver and stationmaster was infectious.' So recorded the *Dundee Courier* in an interesting aside, and one can imagine that the LNER staff must have been delighted to await the arrival of road vehicles bringing the air travellers from Turnhouse airport. Their progress was marred by traffic jams, proving that nothing much changes in transport terms, as any modern airport traveller will confirm if he or she has experienced the congestion in the Corstorphine area of the city.

The 'plane appears to have emerged from an unseasonal deluge of rain and hail to land at Turnhouse in bright sunshine at 5.45 p.m., much to the delight of the drenched crowd. Waverley was reached in the surprisingly fast time of about twenty-five minutes, at around 6.10 p.m, perhaps four minutes after the train's arrival. But this was not how some newspapers saw it. The *Bulletin* and the *Glasgow Herald* both announced that the air-travellers reached Waverley 'just in time to welcome' the train! Indeed, as late as 1966 a Royal Aeronautical Society publication claimed that the 'plane won by fifteen minutes in a 1928 'race between Croydon and Turnhouse'. A similar claim is made in A.J. Jackson's book *British Civil Aircraft since 1919*.

Such inaccuracy was symptomatic of the whole exercise. The LNER was involved in the 'Heads-I-win, tails-you-lose' competition which has become familiar treatment from the media for Britain's railways over the years. The aeroplane was new, exciting and required no small courage to fly in (three out of the seven Argosies were lost in accidents). It was surely unthinkable that it should be beaten to the finishing line by a *steam*-powered train.

The damage done to the LNER's public image by inaccurate and unsympathetic press reporting was surely compounded by the speech now made by that usually sage individual, Sir Ralph Wedgwood. Speaking at the North British Hotel, at a dinner which followed the journey to Edinburgh, Sir Ralph proposed 'Success and prosperity to the Imperial Airways', looking forward to future competition 'without apprehension, even with pleasure'. He saw the two types of transport as 'complementary rather than competitive', with air travel helping rail transport.

Everyone is entitled to be wrong now and again, but in retrospect it is difficult to follow the LNER Chief General Manager's reasoning. This was the man, remember, who a few years later had sufficient vision and confidence in his Chief Mechanical Engineer, to encourage Gresley to introduce high-speed running with streamlined steam engines, when a diesel railcar service was being proposed between London and Newcastle. It was Wedgwood too, who insisted that Haymarket crewmen be given the opportunity to undertake express duties on the ECML south of Berwick, thus introducing Edinburgh's 'Enginemen Elite' (as Norman McKillop was later to call them), to rival the best efforts of their colleagues at King's Cross, Grantham and Gateshead. What a pity he did not feel similarly enterprising in calling Imperial's bluff.

For bluff it undoubtedly was. The Imperial press releases made a 3-hour city centre to city centre journey time seem quite feasible – nearly five hours faster than the train, hampered by its wretched 1896 restriction – but Imperial had not exactly proved that it could be done. Major Mealing, an Air Ministry official who travelled on the flight, more realistically advised the press that the plane could 'save $2\frac{1}{2}$ hours' on the train's timing, including a thirty-minute boarding period at Croydon. (Interestingly, by 1937 Railway Air Services was offering a five hours, twenty-five minutes city centre London–Glasgow service, indicating the dubiety of the 1928 Imperial claim.) Not only that, if some passengers suffered air sickness in a comparatively sedate flight made in what was largely fine summer weather, what would a winter flight be like? And how reliable would the service have been, with fog or crosswinds to hinder take-offs and landings? Perhaps the far-seeing Sir Ralph was already anticipating a rail-air link-up some six years before it actually took place – but even such diplomacy hardly justifies the extravagant claims that Imperial were being allowed to get away with.

Would a speed challenge between air and rail have been so impossible for rail to win between London and Edinburgh on a 'one off' basis in 1928? Even if the LNER had exceeded Imperial's passenger complement by as much as 100 per cent, a three-coach Pullman train could have been run between the cities in six hours or less. Bear in mind too that the *City of Glasgow* had been reduced by headwinds to a 30 mph pace for one part of its journey northwards, prompting Major Mealing's realism. Not only that, but Imperial 'cheated' by starting from Croydon: had the flight started from King's Cross or from a point equidistant between there and Croydon as, say, Trafalgar Square or the Savoy, a road journey of ten miles or more would have been added to the intrepid air passenger's journey, and in central London – even in mid-morning – that could have added forty minutes to their journey time.

'We have not discovered what this flight was intended to demonstrate', remarked the *Railway Gazette* when it was all over. Nevertheless, the 1928 non-race was an advertising triumph for Imperial. The LNER's self-satisfied complacency did them no credit. That their staff privately looked on the Imperial initiative as a challenge, is evidenced by the heading of the relevant LNER file dealing with the matter. It was entitled 'Air Challenge to the Railways'.

The file consists of newspaper cuttings, including many illustrations. All the pictures feature the aeroplane; the 'Flying Scotsman' does not appear in any of them. If Imperial was waging a war in terms of public relations, it had beaten the LNER literally out of sight.

No passports, No customs: Non-Stop to 1939

By 22 September 1928, 125 runs had been made non-stop in each direction between London and Edinburgh, a total mileage for the 250 trips of 98,165. Needless to say, this cumulative distance was completed with only one unpunctual arrival! On 14 August a traction engine fouled the down line at the Northumbrian village of Chathill, causing a thirty-one-minute late arrival at Waverley for the express. A second unpunctual journey might have been expected on 7 September when No. 2580 *Shotover*, heroine of the first day's operations, failed at Grantham, being replaced by No. 2561 *Minoru*. But Driver Pibworth – who had taken the first northbound 'Non-Stop' out of King's Cross, made a mockery of the schedule by making up twenty-two minutes, arriving at the London terminus early.

Gresley had designed a new articulated dining car set for the 'Flying Scotsman', but it was not available for the beginning of the non-stop season in May 1928. In fact it was to be 16 July when the new sets went into service on the train, attracting considerable acclamation from the technical press and an appreciative public. The triplet set, mounted on four bogies, had internal styling by Sir Charles Allom, designed to emulate Louis XVI-period décor. There were no ceiling lights, artificial lighting being supplied from behind luminous pelmets over the side windows. First class saloons in soft blue and stone, and red and stone flanked a fully-electric kitchen car, along with a Third class dining car in green and stone.

The summer of 1928 was significant for marking the introduction of the first batch of A3 Pacifics ready-built with the improved valve arrangements. Numbered 2743–52 and delivered between August 1928 and April 1929, they came to be regarded by many observers as the best of the class (a later batch of which was still building into early 1935). One of the new A3s was No. 2750 *Papyrus*, unusually eulogized in H.C. Webster's book *2750: Legend of a Locomotive*:

> One of those creations of man which by a happy combination of design and workmanship and good fortune are so outstanding in performance and so sweet to handle that they become a legend.

But it was one of the earlier engines which caught the eye as the first summer of non-stop operations continued into an uneasy autumn, with the LNER and LMS eyeing

A locomotive legend, A3 No. 2750 *Papyrus* is seen at Hatfield on an unidentified up express in the early 1930s. The subject of a book praising her work on the ECML, *Papyrus* was the last non-streamlined Pacific to head a regular non-stop train between London and Edinburgh. (Photomatic)

each other's long-distance aspirations and achievements. For no fewer than fifty-five days Gateshead's No. 2569 *Gladiateur* ran a punishing two-day, 785 mile roster on long-distance expresses between Newcastle, London and Edinburgh, including a down 'Scotsman' throughout the length of its journey. Meanwhile, the LMS was running its its 'Royal Scot' express with an additional stop at Crewe.

Thanks to the LNER, 'Non-Stop' running became the 'in phrase' in railway marketing. In 1929 the Southern advertised the 'Bournemouth Limited' with the words '108 miles *Non Stop* in Two Hours!', while both the *Railway Magazine* and *Railway Gazette* reported on the Great Western's newly-accelerated 'Cheltenham Flyer' as 'a record non-stop train'. Yet London to Bournemouth hardly rates as an odyssey of inordinate length and surely the real fame of the GWR express at that time lay in accomplishing its Swindon–Paddington seventy-seven-mile dash in seventy minutes start-to-stop at an average booked speed of 66.2 mph. This was Britain's fastest train, soon to become even faster; yet even highly-respected specialist magazines dubbed the speedster with a 'non-stop' label. The fact was, simply, that the rail industry had a new advertising gimmick.

The 1929 season of non-stop running began on 8 July, the traditional time of year for the introduction of the summer timetable. From Hungarian artist Ladislas Freiwirth, the LNER commissioned an imaginative motif of an A3 with lightning sparking from its cylinders to advertise the relaunch of the service. Yet it was again to be the LMS which would end the year with another long-distance record.

Still in her original A1 form, No. 2566 *Ladas* is seen in 1938 at Eastfield depot, in her hometown of Glasgow, where she was built by the North British Loco Company in 1924. When operating from Edinburgh's Haymarket depot this engine headed the inaugural up 'Flying Scotsman' in 1929, the second year of non-stop operations. (Photomatic)

One rail writer (P.N. Townend) has suggested that this year's service on the LNER got off to an unfortunate start with one of the first day's 'Scotsman' services having to stop for water. This is not borne out by a perusal of the contemporary press, which recorded that both trains arrived early, the down service reaching Waverley at six minutes past six, the up, powered by No. 2566 *Ladas*, arriving at King's Cross seven minutes later. Of course, with no speeding-up of the schedule, it was quite possible that a stop had been made for water without preventing an early arrival. King's Cross rostered new faces to the duty; Messrs Toplis and Lostin for the first part of the down journey, Perry and Benby for the southern half of the southbound. Henderson and Collins of Haymarket ran the first part of the up train, waved off by Chief General Manager Sir Ralph Wedgwood, with Gateshead's 1928 team of Smith and Bambra taking responsibility for the northern section of the down service.

The new batch of A3s was already establishing a considerable reputation as being the best of the class, No. 2750 *Papyrus* showing its credentials on 23 May with the run already mentioned in which Driver Gutteridge and Fireman Roberts made up twenty-seven minutes on the up 10.00. Not slow to realize the public's potential interest in speed and timekeeping, the LNER invited 'Scotsman' passengers to record passing times, with a 'sweep' on estimated times for passing particular places. Six prizes were awarded on each journey – three to each sex, for no obvious reason.

But if the LNER was content to make the non-stop 'Flying Scotsman' the flagship of its passenger services, the LMS once again turned a long-distance, non-stop train into a buccaneering privateer. This time the record captured was the longest southbound,

For nearly twenty years this locomotive, 'Royal Scot' 4-6-0 No. 6127 *Novelty* (later re-named *Old Contemptibles*), held the non-stop record for a southbound journey (395 miles). That occurred in 1929, as related in the accompanying text. Sole driver on that occasion was David Gibson of Polmadie, seen standing next to the cylinder of this Glasgow-built engine. (R.B. Haddon collection, Mitchell Library)

non-stop train journey in Britain. Its starting place bore the scarcely picturesque name of Glenboig.

Glenboig was a mining township some six miles north-east of Glasgow, with, at that time, a station on the Law Junction–Greenhill Junction line (effectively the former Caledonian main line between Carlisle and Aberdeen bypassing Glasgow) just north of the junction with the Glasgow (Buchanan Street)–Aberdeen link. In order to mark the opening of the new Bussey coal distillation works, the LMS arranged a special train for 120 passengers from Euston to the site. This comprised sleeper stock, departing Euston on 19 July at fifteen minutes past midnight. The immediate destination was the halt-like station at Lanark Racecourse where the guests transferred, at some ungodly hour, to daytime stock, breakfasting on the way to Glenboig. This second train formation (including two cinema vans) was used for the return journey to Euston – another record run for a company which hardly owned the correct equipment for such operations, but simply didn't know when it was beaten.

Leaving Glenboig at 11.30, the eleven-coach rake was headed by 'Royal Scot' No. 6127 *Novelty* in the charge of Driver Gibson of Polmadie, one of the heroes of the 1928 dash with *Cameronian*. (There seems to be no record of a second driver rostered to the duty, and only one driver – David Gibson – was photographed at the Euston arrival ceremony. His was a magnificent feat of railroading endurance.) London was reached at 19.28 after a non-stop run of 395½ miles, again beating the 'Flying Scotsman', this time by some three miles.

There was no reply from the LNER, which maintained its business-like policy of regarding non-stop operations as an integral part of the overall express passenger pattern – more's the pity! With a replacement crew, a generous coal supply and some judicious nursing of the injectors, surely a 'one-off' Glasgow version of the 'Scotsman' could have been run through to Glasgow (Queen Street) via Waverley to answer the LMS's challenge. It would have meant a final leg of nearly 120 miles without water replenishment, but even a stop for water anywhere on the Edinburgh–Glasgow line west of Winchburgh Junction, would have constituted a world record. After all, the principal reason for such long-distance operation was to capture publicity, was it not?

'Sans arrêt' were the words highlighted in neon above the Gare du Nord in Paris in the spring of 1930. They announced the non-stop running of a Paris–Liege service in exactly four hours over a distance of 367 km (about 230 miles), for a limited period only. If not a record-breaker, it proved that 'Non-Stop' was not just a British travel fixation. Significantly this continental example included the crossing of a frontier more international than Lamberton Toll at Berwick or the Sark bridge at Gretna.

It is interesting to notice that, irrespective of the limits of British geography, the LMS and LNER seemed to be capable of longer non-stop express operations than their counterparts overseas. In France the longest regular journeys around this time were the Est company's four-times daily services from Paris to Nancy – a run of 219 miles. Most creditably however, it was achieved without water-troughs, these being installed only on the Etat system at the time.

A3 Pacific No. 2746 *Fairway* seen at Doncaster in July 1935. This locomotive headed the inaugural down 'Flying Scotsman' service for the summer of 1930. (Photomatic)

The only non-Pacific locomotive ever to run a 'Non-Stop' express on the East Coast main line was LNER Class W1 4–6–4 No. 10000, which did so only twice. She is seen here passing Hadley Wood with the down 'Flying Scotsman' on 1 August 1930, uniquely crewed by two sets of men from the same shed – Gateshead (Newcastle). (A.L.P. Reavil)

The summer non-stop running of 1930 – on the East Coast only, the West Coast refraining from its one-off histrionics for the first time in three years – began on 7 July. The *Railway Observer* reported that No. 4472 *Flying Scotsman* headed the first up train, in a variation of the usual operational pattern, with No. 2746 *Fairway* taking the first down service.

By the end of that summer season the LNER was able to announce that the 'Flying Scotsman' had been run non-stop without a single case of locomotive failure. A total of 51,386 miles had been traversed, comprising 132 trips, with only one late arrival, and that not attributable to the locomotives or crews.

A particularly eminent performer on the service was the new A3 No. 2795 *Call Boy* of Haymarket, running continuously for twenty-eight days on the 'Scotsman', all but four of them non-stop, the other four days being the corresponding Sunday service which stopped intermediately. No. 2795 was one of a new batch of eight A3s numbered 2595–9 and 2795–7 introduced that year. The first five were allocated to Gateshead, while the other three went to Haymarket, the first two of these, Nos. 2795/6, being the only engines of the batch to boast corridor tenders.

The year was unusual in seeing the only known case of a non-Pacific locomotive allocated to an entire 'Non-Stop' duty on the East Coast line. On 31 July, rail enthusiasts, or 'spotters' as the younger among them were not afraid to be called, saw a most un-Pacific front end emerge from Gasworks tunnel and lead the up 'Flying Scotsman' into King's Cross at the end of its 393 mile journey. This was 4–6–4 'Hush

hush' No. 10000, an experimental design by Gresley incorporating a Yarrow water-tube boiler pressed to 450 psi. The unusual front-end was the result of eliminating the conventional chimney due to the necessity for one of the steam drums to be mounted as high as possible within the loading gauge. Four cylinders, two high-pressure between the frames and two low-pressure outside, powered the usual 6 ft 8 in driving wheels.

Painted battleship grey, No. 10000 was classified W1 but was not to be an ultimate success. Cecil J. Allen commented on the black smoke which 'poured ceaselessly' from its chimney (or the place where the chimney was expected to be) and recorded an uneventful run behind this engine on the 'Scotsman' during its stopping timetable. Within seven years, No. 10000 was rebuilt with an A4 front end but retained its specially-built corridor tender, which interestingly held twenty-nine gallons more than those already in service, until 1948. Its up journey on the 'Non-Stop' on 31 July 1930, and the down journey the following day, were the only occasions it, or any other non-Pacific, was rostered for this duty. Unusually, the down journey on 1 August involved two Gateshead crews, drivers J. Gascoigne and J.G. Eltringham and firemen H.A. Brayson and J.W.P. Ritchie.

The summer of 1931 was the last when the 'Flying Scotsman' adhered to its ridiculously protracted 8¼-hour schedule, which slightly diminishes the otherwise excellent statistics the LNER released about its timekeeping. By the time non-stop running ceased for the season on 14 September, eighteen crews had driven eight engines on a total aggregate of 37,728 miles non-stop. Not a single minute was lost.

As already mentioned, 1932 was to be a watershed in the history of Anglo-Scottish railway operations. At last, the 1896 agreement, designed to prevent racing, was discontinued, as it should have been years before. The LNER and LMS were free to re-time their trains between London and Edinburgh/Glasgow in accordance with the parameters of the technology available and of safety requirements. There was even a hint of co-operation between the two companies, with steps being taken later that year to introduce some degree of interchangeability of LMS and LNER tickets on each others' lines.

The summer began brightly with an acceleration for the 'Flying Scotsman' in the May intermediate timetable. Twenty-five minutes was wiped from the schedule in each direction, but even better was to come with the opening of the non-stop 'season' from 18 July. The timing for the famous express was now 7½ hours – it would be the crawling Scotsman no longer! The relief 'Junior Scotsman' was re-timetabled at seven hours fifty minutes for the same journey, with intermediate stops.

This was what railway author Ken Hoole was later to describe as 'the most momentous period in the history of the East Coast main line', and this was undoubtedly true of the pre-diesel era. Until the outbreak of war in 1939, travel on the East Coast was to be become faster, and no less punctual, than ever before. As flagship of the line, the 'Flying Scotsman' spearheaded the improvement, even if it was to become eclipsed by the later streamlined trains. Its working arrangements in 1932 are worth examining.

The timetable improvement was very much the result of accelerations south of the Tyne. Five hours were now scheduled for the King's Cross–Newcastle run, 268 miles in 300 minutes, start to pass. The hardest running was reserved for the former Great Northern section. Peterborough, seventy-six miles out from the capital, had to be passed northbound in seventy-nine minutes, with the twenty-seven mile Hitchin–Huntingdon

The summer timetable and resumption of the non-stop service on 18 July 1932, appropriately with No. 4472 *Flying Scotsman*. The engine is about to leave King's Cross at the head of the northbound train. (Hulton Picture Company)

stretch being timetabled at twenty-two minutes – an average of 73½ mph. Doncaster, 155 miles out, was scheduled to be passed in 170 minutes, with the York–Darlington section of the line timed at slightly less than 60 mph in forty-seven minutes for the forty-four miles, pass to pass.

In contrast, north of Newcastle there was time to spare; 150 minutes for the 124½ miles. It could well be that the high speeds south of Grantham were necessary to keep the 'Scotsman' ahead of its own relief, but the comparatively slow timing on the northern section indicated that there was still fat on the bone.

A week before the non-stop services began for the summer, the Locomotive Running Superintendents for each of the LNER's three areas issued a joint memorandum containing instructions for the crews of the 'Flying Scotsman'. It can still be consulted in the Public Record Office, and today's reader can only be amazed at how untechnical it is. A modern car or computer comes supplied with a factual, often impenetrable manual; the working of Britain's most important long-distance train in 1932 is a veritable leaflet in comparison!

Beginning with the solemn advice that each crew was to carry an extra firing shovel, the memo confirmed 'at or near Tollerton' as the change-over point. In the event of failure to pick up enough water at Danby Wiske or Lucker troughs – the only ones between Edinburgh and Doncaster – stops were to be made at Alnmouth and/or Darlington in the up direction, and Thirsk and/or Alnmouth in the case of the down train. More interesting was the information about pilot (i.e. standby) locomotives for use in case of the failure of the locomotive on the road.

Pacifics were to stand by at King's Cross, Grantham, Doncaster, York and Newcastle in the down direction, with Atlantics as pilots at Hitchin, Peterborough, Darlington and Tweedmouth. The up 'Scotsman' would have Pacific power in reserve at Edinburgh, Newcastle, Doncaster and Grantham only; Atlantics would stand by at Tweedmouth, Darlington, York, Peterborough and Hitchin. Notice that, despite its lack of Pacifics at this time, York depot was having to arrange for two standby engines simultaneously, each facing in opposite directions. Not surprisingly, an Atlantic comprised at least one of the covering engines at this approximate half-way point. What is particularly interesting is that an Atlantic was being officially rostered for standby for the up train, on the most strictly scheduled part of the 'Flying Scotsman's' route; presumably this was considered less of a problem than the difficult logistics of water replenishment on the down journey, where a borrowed Pacific was thought necessary as reserve.

The standby Atlantics were Ivatt C1s in the case of the former GNR depots south of, and including, York. Three of this class were allocated to York in 1932, where a number of Raven C7s of the former North Eastern Railway were also based. There is a record of one of the later streamlined trains taking a C7 southwards from York, following the failure of the usual A4, but the driver exchanged it for a C1, with which he was more familiar, at Doncaster. North of York, C7s, the old North Eastern Z class, were the usual standby locomotives at most of the specified points, including Tweedmouth, which had received an allocation specially for this duty in 1930. Darlington, however, maintained the older C6s for this task in the years immediately after 1928.

The memo specified that, in the event of breakdown before the change-over point was reached, both sets of crew were to travel on the footplate from the location where the replacement engine took over. This would surely guarantee an uncomfortable journey on, say, an Atlantic footplate north from Peterborough, or up from Tweedmouth, with no (official) facilities for a meal over the remaining six or seven hours. It seems a fairly heartless regulation given that speed would normally be low through York station, in whose environs a quick emergency change-over could be made. Yet within fifteen months, two crews were to travel from Grantham to Edinburgh in the cab of a Pacific and make up twenty-two minutes on schedule into the bargain, as will be related later.

The new accelerated non-stop season began with LNER Chairman William Whitelaw seeing off the up 'Scotsman' from Waverley on 18 July. It was headed by A3 No. 2795 *Call Boy* driven by Haymarket's Sandy Davidson, who despite his splendidly Scottish name, was another former North Eastern man. The other three crewmen were not recorded. At King's Cross the redoubtable Driver Sparshatt had to cope with the ballyhoo of being photographed in the company of such celebrities as Sir Malcolm Campbell, the road speed ace, before he set No. 4472 to the northern road.

Rail historian O.S. Nock was privileged to travel on the footplate of No. 2795 *Call Boy* on the down 'Scotsman' shortly after the introduction of the accelerated schedule. Visiting the 'spick and span' cab when the train was already some six hours out from

This photograph taken around 1959 shows A3 No. 60099 *Call Boy* when equipped with double chimney, a development which gave the class an added lease of life. This Haymarket-based engine headed the inaugural down 'Flying Scotsman' of 1932, the first to be scheduled non-stop at less than 8¼ hours. (Photomatic)

London, he noted that the near-500 ton load was proving no problem for the engine which had plenty of coal left and was 'purring along' on 15 per cent cut-off and less than full regulator. This was in marked contrast to a post-war journey he made when A4s were powering the train, and the two show the contrasting and, to some extent, unpredictable nature of steam power, even when it was represented by well-designed, well-maintained machines driven by experienced crews.

One July afternoon in 1932, railway enthusiast Gerald Spink was waiting to see the non-stop 'Flying Scotsman' pass through Newcastle Central, when he was surprised to notice that the train, already some ninety seconds late, was slowing to a stop. The King's Cross Pacific heading the 'Scotsman' had run hot; a replacement engine was needed immediately. Fortunately, Gateshead's No. 2573 *Harvester* was waiting to back down onto a later train and was hurriedly coupled in place of its failed sister. It took all of six minutes, with the crew even having time to transfer the smokebox headboard to the replacement. Despite leaving Central some 7½ minutes late *Harvester* apparently had no difficulty in reaching Edinburgh on time with an eleven coach load, confirming the comparatively easy schedule on this stretch.

Indeed, despite its long-overdue acceleration, the 'Flying Scotsman' was still not as fast between the capitals as one East Coast train in 1896, the 8 p.m. ex-King's Cross, which was scheduled to reach Waverley in seven hours twenty-five minutes overnight, inclusive of three stops.

Mention of the 'Scotsman' headboard is an ideal cue to introduce Eric Gill into the story of the 'Non-Stop'. Gill was an artist and calligrapher commissioned to design a standardized form of lettering for all of the LNER's printed material, stationery and advertising. It was an imaginative initiative by the LNER, a company highly aware of the value of good design as the streamline age of the 1930s was to prove.

Gill Sans lettering replaced Haymarket's improvised lettering on the headboard of the famous express, Gill himself placing the first such board on No. 4475 *Flying Fox* at a ceremony at King's Cross on 21 November 1932. Intriguingly, part of the artist's fee for the job was a footplate trip on the 'Flying Scotsman'.

Gill was allowed to travel with the crew of No. 2582 *Sir Hugo* on the King's Cross – Grantham section of the 'Scotsman's' northbound run during the winter timetable, when a stop was made at Grantham. From there the artist returned to London on the footplate of the even more illustrious No. 2750 *Papyrus*. Gill wrote about his experiences for the *LNER Magazine*, and his comments about the manual firing of these famous steam locomotives are worth recording here.

It's surprising how these primitive (firing) methods persist . . . Here we were on an engine of the most powerful kind in the world (sic), attached to one of the most famous of all travelling hotels – a string of coaches called The Flying Scotsman – with its Cocktail Bar and Beauty parlours, its dining saloons, decorated in more or less credible imitation of the salons of eighteenth century France, its waiters and guards and attendants of all sorts, its ventilation and heating apparatus as efficient as those of the Strand Palace Hotel, and here we were carrying on as if we were pulling a string of coal trucks.

This is a timely reminder that the punctuality of the 'Flying Scotsman' was, ultimately, dependent on the sheer strength and stamina of two men shovelling their share of up to nine tons of coal into a furnace almost without a break for more than four hours each. Not only that, but even when his shift was over, the first fireman on the 'Non-Stop' was sometimes asked to return to help his replacement on the footplate if the engine was shy for steam. The firemen themselves were not unaware of the social inequality illustrated by the comparison between the train's passengers and its crew, particularly when there might appear to be little difference between tare and gross weights of trains operating at any except peak times. There was an obvious implication that the companies were adding passenger facilities without any consideration of the increase in manual effort such facilities would cause. Adding to tare weights was the rigid class convention which demanded that First and Third class passengers should have separate dining-cars. In 1930 a fireman wrote to the *Railway Magazine* commenting: 'For a fireman to have to heave coal into these monsters when trailing enormous trains of 30-ton to 34-ton bogies about, with a few passengers in each, is a heart-breaking job.'

There is simply no comparison with modern transport methods, where acceleration or hill-climbing ability can be acquired simply by moving a lever. It plays nonsense too, with horsepower calculations and drawbar formulae. The steam locomotive was a labour-intensive machine, requiring the constant contribution of human toil.

After the comparatively easy timetabling of the non-stop 'Flying Scotsman' over the previous four years, enthusiasts must have waited with interest for the annual release of official information on the train's punctuality following the introduction of a much stricter schedule in 1932.

The LNER obliged with the following information: a total of ninety-six non-stop runs had been made in both directions in a season lasting from 18 July to 11 September. Forty-four up journeys were accomplished on or before time; two of the four late arrivals were less than five minutes to the bad, and there had been one each of seven and forty-five minutes. This last was caused when No. 2547 *Doncaster* ran hot. In the other direction, there had been only two late arrivals, each of only one minute. One of these was incurred when a replacement engine had had to be found for No. 4476 *Royal Lancer* which developed a hot middle small end at Newcastle, where a stop of five minutes was necessary to change engines. This sounds remarkably like the incident described by Dr Spink, who believed the Edinburgh arrival to have been punctual, but these could have been two quite separate incidents; all part of a magnificent record of timekeeping of around 94 per cent punctuality over a world-record distance, through a densely-trafficked network.

The year 1933 arrived with No. 2750 *Papyrus* producing another amazing run in which an eighteen-coach, 615-ton express was hurried from Grantham to King's Cross, 105 miles, in 115 minutes, this including a signal delay of at least three minutes, and with the twenty-seven miles between Huntingdon and Hitchin reeled off in one second under twenty-five minutes. C.J. Allen was remarkably unlavish in his praise of *Papyrus* when he said of the run, 'I know of no equal effort on the part of a Gresley Pacific recorded previously.'

Gresley's Pacifics were amassing an unsurpassed reputation for powerful performances at high speed, their mettle shining all the more visibly because of the increased amount of quadrupled track, offering refuges for slower trains without passing on delays to the expresses. By 1933, for example, only the six miles between Pilmoor and Thirsk were not furnished with relief lines on the thirty-mile stretch between York and Northallerton.

The public awareness of this speed explosion is best illustrated by an incident in the early 1930s when Allen, watching the arrival of a fast Leeds express at King's Cross, had two detailed logs of the run just completed thrust into his hands there and then, with another three following in the post!

With the GWR slashing the timetable of the lightweight 'Cheltenham Flyer' to a booked average approaching 80 mph, and the Germans about to introduce a high-speed diesel service between Berlin and Hamburg from 15 May, the potential for a fast LNER service was gaining prominence. Interestingly, Driver Sparshatt of King's Cross had driven No. 2547 *Doncaster* at the head of an unusually light 250-ton train from Peterborough to London in just sixty-six minutes, inclusive of a signal delay at New Southgate, a few days before Christmas 1931. The LNER authorities can have been in no doubt of their engines' potential for hauling lighter, more strictly-timed expresses. Yet the year did not see any major acceleration by the company on its Anglo–Scottish services.

The usual publicity beano accompanied the first departure of the northbound 'Flying Scotsman' from King's Cross on 17 July 1933. This time Driver Sparshatt found himself shaking hands, for the benefit of the cameras, with Captain G. de Havilland, the recent winner of the King's Cup Air Race. The LNER Publicity Department certainly could not be faulted for effort! Fireman Smith made up the other half of the southern crew, but the

One of the lesser-known records of non-stop running on the East Coast main line was held by Class A3 Pacific No. 60057 *Ormonde*. In 1933, when numbered 2556, she substituted for No. 4472 *Flying Scotsman* on the down train of the same name over the 288 miles between Grantham and Edinburgh. Not being fitted with a corridor tender, she embarked two crews in her cab for the journey, during which she cut twenty-two minutes from the schedule. In this mid-1950s picture, *Ormonde* is seen approaching Longniddry with the down 'Scotsman'. (D.A. Anderson)

engine's identity was not recorded – it was probably No. 4472 as usual. From the northern end, Driver Shedden and Fireman Stuart had nothing more trying than the chairman to cope with before heading south on the footplate of No. 2796 *Spearmint*.

The record non-stop running of 1933 had a glorious climax. On the last down journey, No. 4472 *Flying Scotsman* – still an unconverted A1 – developed a hot big end and came off the train at Grantham. Sister engine No. 2556 *Ormonde* substituted but, having no corridor tender, embarked both sets of crews in the cab, as regulations required. None other than Driver Sparshatt and his (un-named) fireman took the controls to begin with, before being replaced by Driver Dron and an unknown mate when the usual change-over point was reached in Yorkshire. Meanwhile time was steadily being made up. The twelve coach train left Grantham nineteen minutes late, passed York fourteen minutes down, but had halved the deficit by Newcastle. Edinburgh was not reached punctually – *Ormonde* brought the train in three minutes early! Cecil M. Furst, in reporting this extraordinary achievement to the railway press, estimated a nett time of seven hours five minutes. It was almost certainly a long-distance record (288 miles) for a non-stop run on the East Coast main-line for a locomotive without a corridor tender.

However, 1933 saw the LMS introduce its first Pacific, Stanier's No. 6200 *The Princess Royal*, and it was not long before she and her sister No. 6201 *Princess Elizabeth*, began working the up 'Royal Scot' and a corresponding down working on a single roster between Carlisle and Euston. This 600-mile round trip was already being run daily by the smaller 'Royal Scot' 4–6–0s, and it would be ungracious not to record such a daily achievement as this. Soon the new Pacifics were working throughout on a daily roster between Euston and Glasgow, although not non-stop – yet.

While 1933 saw no accelerations to speak of on the LNER's main line, a process of quiet consolidation was taking place. In contrast, 1934 showed that Gresley was not finished as a locomotive designer of stunning originality.

Cock o' the North and its sister P2 2–8–2s have no real place in the non-stop story. They lacked corridor tenders and were in any event designed for service on the difficult ex-NBR line between Edinburgh and Aberdeen. Nor were they to have an altogether illustrious career; although they showed an astonishing ability to haul heavy loads at speed, they were to come under something of a cloud during the war years and were rebuilt by Gresley's unsympathetic successor, Edward Thompson. Their role in the story of Britain's non-stop express services probably lies in the streamlined internal steam passages they incorporated. Both this detail, plus the sheer overall confidence manifested in their highly unusual external appearance, was a confirmation that Gresley was working towards his *pièce de résistance* – the A4.

Streamlining was the coming fashion in transport, in architecture, even in interior décor. The railway press contained illustrations and information in 1934 of monstrous continental locomotives encased in insect-like armour which bore, in one particular German proposal, an uncomfortable similarity to the Alien of the 1970s film of that name!

But steam was by no means being replaced by the new concept of diesel railcars, despite the successful advent of the latter in Germany. Operating diesels on an otherwise exclusively steam-orientated railway system produced unexpectedly disappointing availability figures for the German State Railways, as BR was also later to learn. Although the diesel railcar could connect Berlin and Hamburg (178 miles apart) in 138 minutes, steam power was required to deputize when the diesel was unavailable. It was soon discovered that a conventional Class O3 four-cylinder Pacific could do the same journey in 150 minutes, hauling three coaches carrying 132 First class and 144 Second class passengers. Similarly, French steam power was found to be a successful replacement for the two-hour service over the 136 miles between Paris and Deauville. Gresley must have been watching all this with interest at this stage, although he would not be alone in wondering if such light high-speed trains could be injected into the bloodstream of a densely-trafficked rail system such as the LNER's.

Such was the interest in streamlining that non-stop running became *passé*. There were fewer references to the summer 'Flying Scotsman' in the railway press, although the statistics for the 1934 season were impressive enough. Out of sixty down arrivals all but one were punctual or early; 3 September had seen a loss of thirty-two minutes owing to an engine failure at Longniddry, barely twenty miles short of the destination. In the up direction, there were three late arrivals at King's Cross.

But who was interested in tortoises (admittedly a moderately accelerated one) in the age of the hare? Indeed, non-stop running was not to recapture the public's imagination until after the Second World War, proving that high speed will surpass non-stop operations as a public attraction any time.

We cannot leave British non-stop running in 1934 without noticing two facts. One was that Railway Air Services began flying between Croydon and Glasgow daily from 20 August. The original route included touch-downs at Birmingham, Manchester, Isle of Man and Belfast, with Liverpool and Belfast the only stops from November (the latter involving a change to another aircraft). The time taken was around $5\frac{1}{2}$ hours (inclusive of transport to and from city centres); obviously there was scope for the railway services to look hard but positively at their own potential for acceleration, even allowing for the rail companies' own participation in the new air company. If any justification was required for the new 'fad' of streamlining, here it was.

The second story from 1934 concerns a lady passenger travelling from Aberdeen to Darlington on an August morning. On arrival from the north at Waverley station, Edinburgh, she failed to realize that she was seated in the through portion which was being attached to the non-stop 'Flying Scotsman' and unwittingly began a journey which was to take her non-stop through her destination, altogether some 464 miles out of her way! A steward on the train discovered the lady's plight and had a quiet word with the driver waiting in the first coach to take over the train just north of York. Realizing that the errant passenger's last chance to reach Darlington that day was to catch the 5.30 p.m. departure from King's Cross – the scheduled arrival time of the 'Scotsman' itself – the London-based driver deliberately ran ahead of schedule, pulling up at King's Cross with five minutes to spare. It showed a concept of public service that has somehow long disappeared. Whether the lady passenger had to pay an excess fare is not recorded.

Nineteen thirty-four commands a special place in the story of non-stop long-distance running in international, if not British, terms. On 26 May 1934, the diesel-powered 'Burlington Zephyr' ran from Denver (Colorado) to Chicago – all of 1,015 miles – without a stop.

There was little comparison between the then current concept of a British express train, with its heavy coaches transporting (in theory) hundreds of passengers between points A and B, compared with the new 'Zephyr'. In contrast, the Chicago, Burlington and Quincy Railroad (since 1970, part of the Burlington Northern Line) envisaged operating a lightweight high-speed service between Kansas City and the Nebraskan cities of Omaha and Lincoln. The result was a three-coach, stainless steel rail-car set mounted on four bogies, the Budd-built diesel developing 600 hp, quite sufficient to propel its own tare weight of 87 tons plus the burden of seventy-two passengers.

From the time of the diesel's construction, the company had intended to exhibit it in the 'Wings of the Century' transport pageant at the Chicago World's Fair but, with considerable imagination, arranged for it to travel all the way to the fair from Denver non-stop in a record time. This was the equivalent of travelling from London to Aberdeen and back again in British terms, but the Americans had to contend with one practical consideration which thankfully has never been a problem for Britain's main-line railways. Between Denver and Chicago there were no fewer than 1,070 public and 619 private road crossings of the track: every single one of these had to be staffed for the occasion of the run! If the reports are true that two men were hired to hold up road traffic at each and every crossing, then the CBQ Railroad was employing no fewer than 3,378 men specially for this purpose!

The logistics of it all were impressive, and fraught with potential problems. Not only had the crossings flagmen to be trained, placed at their locations and kept notified of the train's progress, but track engineers had to post temporary speed restriction signs at problem areas of the track. Obviously, a run faster than the usual twenty-six hours was envisaged, and in the event the 'Zephyr' let nobody down.

Leaving Denver's Union Street Station at 5.05 a.m. (Mountain Time, the two cities were so far apart as to be in different time-zones), the diesel reeled off the distance in thirteen hours five minutes forty-four seconds, before coming to rest for the first time at Chicago's Halsted Street at 7.10 p.m. Central Time. 'Bedlam broke loose', according to American railway historian Freeman Hubbard, as the 'Zephyr' rolled to a halt on a specially-prepared display area before a packed audience. (Shades of Francis Webb's plan to run non-stop from Euston to a special grandstand in Edinburgh in 1890.) The average speed had been 77.6 mph with a maximum of $112\frac{1}{4}$ mph for three miles. Over a 401-mile distance, between Denver and Harvard, Nebraska – almost exactly that from Euston to Glasgow – speed averaged 79 mph, an incredible feat for the time, and comparable with modern Inter-City timings.

It emerged later that the record was, however, achieved at the cost of not inconsiderable human suffering. The diesel's starting mechanism shorted at speed, which soon fell to 15 mph, while engineers aboard desperately tried to locate and repair the problem. One man, Roy Baer, apparently achieved the desired result by the daunting expedient of holding two live wires together, being badly burned as he did so. His sacrifice was sufficient to regain speed and allow an alternative circuit to be wired up.

The amount of fuel used was reported at 418 gallons, and the final statistic to report about this unique operation was that an estimated half a million people watched the departure, passing or arrival of the train. It made existing non-stop operations look uninspired in comparison. The diesel unit is now preserved at Chicago's Museum of Science and Industry, even if it is no longer the world non-stop record holder, as we shall see later.

However, Britain's railways, if eclipsed by this achievement (again, be it noted, a 'one off', not a regular undertaking), were not totally outshone. For by the end of 1934 *Flying Scotsman* – the engine not the train – had set another record: the first authenticated 100 mph on British railway tracks.

For years there had been controversy as to whether the GWR 4–4–0 *City of Truro* had really attained 102.3 mph in 1904. Various American and continental claims had been made for higher three-figure maxima by steam locomotives, but these were never confirmed by dynamometer car readings. Indeed, there was a feeling among some locomotive engineers that around 95 mph was the theoretical maximum for a reciprocating steam engine.

On 30 November 1934, running a special 147-ton train from King's Cross to Leeds and back, Driver Sparshatt and No. 4472 put all doubt behind them as they proved conclusively that timings such as Peterborough in one hour and Leeds in a shade over $2\frac{1}{2}$ hours, both from London, were perfectly possible with steam. The trick lay in arranging a trailing load light enough to permit hill-climbing at speed – on Stoke Bank speed had never fallen below 81 mph – while not having it so light that there were dangerous

Silver Link, the pioneer A4 No. 2509, is seen hurtling through Hadley Wood on her northbound press trip on 27 September 1935, when a world record steam traction speed of 112½ mph was twice attained. So successful were the A4s that the LNER extended their use on to other express operations, including the non-stop 'Flying Scotsman' in the summer of 1937. (British Railways)

oscillations in drawbar pull. Two additional coaches had been attached on the return journey, accomplished in 157 minutes for the 185 miles, with the fireman understandably tiring. All this with a locomotive designed thirteen years previously and still running with a 180 psi boiler.

That legend of a locomotive, No. 2750 *Papyrus* confirmed the message with another test run the following 5 March. On this occasion 108 mph was reached – still a British record for a non-streamlined steam engine.

This test took place over the entire King's Cross–Newcastle route intended for the first of the LNER's streamlined answers to the 'Flying Hamburger'. Operated by Driver Gutteridge and Fireman Wightman, *Papyrus* took her seven-coach train north in three minutes less than four hours, and was re-crewed at Newcastle by – who else? – Bill Sparshatt and Fireman Webster. The locomotive had not overheated, and the choice of a fresh crew proved to be a masterstroke. The return journey saw London gained in 232 minutes, amply demonstrating that a four- hour service with a specially streamlined train was perfectly feasible.

Nineteen thirty-five was so much the 'Year of the Hare' that the tortoises were ignored. The *LNER Magazine* was so anticipating the autumn introduction of the 'Silver Jubilee' express that the ritual July send-off of the non-stop 'Flying Scotsman' from King's Cross was not recorded.

Nevertheless, the 'Scotsman' could claim to be second to none when it came to luxury rail travel. The first-class compartments were fully air-conditioned, with the restaurant cars styled, as we have seen, in eighteenth century guise. Hairdressing facilities were still available on the train ('men's haircuts for 1/- [5p], ladies' special shampoo, 2/6d' [12p]), while from 1932 a cocktail bar was included. This served Martinis or the 'Flying Scotsman's' own cocktail for 1s. 6d. (7p), while for the equivalent of ten present-day pence (probably £1.50 allowing for inflation) the passenger could purchase a 'Corpse Reviver' cocktail, no doubt to assist in overcoming the effects of any previous evening's libations! Beers were most definitely not on tap.

Passengers could even use the train's own headed notepaper and envelopes when catching up on their correspondence during the journey. That is assuming they were not too busy watching the passing landscape, which the LNER assured them included 'magnificent coast scenery between Newcastle and Edinburgh'. As an aid to viewing this, the train formation was made up, whenever practicable, with the corridor on the west side of the train, to facilitate the eastwards view.

Seven and a half hours were still required for the non-stop schedule between London and Edinburgh, and resulting criticism was not slow in coming from at least one railway journalist that year, C.J. Allen arguing that six hours twenty minutes should be a practical possibility for a non-stop journey. His justification for this was to unite the King's Cross–York timing for the 'Scarborough Flyer' – then the fastest between the two cities – with that of the not over-fast 9.38 a.m. York to Edinburgh. This hypothetical hybrid of existing but quite separate schedules gave a six hour fifty-seven minute timing between London and Edinburgh inclusive of a five-minute stop at Newcastle. But Allen's bold arguments went for nought; the LNER was too heavily locked into the preparations for Britain's first streamlined train.

An historic date in the history of the LNER was 27 September 1935. Exactly 110 years to the day since the Stockton and Darlington Railway had begun passenger-carrying operations, a press run was held of the new 'Silver Jubilee' express between King's Cross and Grantham. This was the first time the public had seen the brand-new, silver-grey A4 Pacific No. 2509 *Silver Link* united with its specially-constructed coaching stock. However, its appearance was only half the attraction!

The run which followed was one of the most outstanding in British railway history in the age of steam, with no fewer than four world records being broken. A record maximum speed of 112½ mph was reached twice and the forty-one miles from Hatfield to Huntingdon run at an average of slightly over 100 mph. Driver Taylor and Fireman Luty were the men responsible, timed by Nigel Gresley himself with what the railway press described as a 'split-second chronograph of vast dimensions'.

Spectacular record-breaking activities apart, more important was the fact that the 'Jubilee' entered regular railway service without any major hitches, operated by *Silver Link* alone for the first fortnight at an average speed of 67 mph for the 536-mile round trip. Rail enthusiasts were not slow to notice that the four new A4s being built for the service were coupled to corridor tenders. Did the LNER plan some future conversion of the 'Scotsman' to streamlined status, they wondered? Although a second order was soon to be placed for A4s, the original batch were, when not allocated to 'Silver Jubilee' workings, rostered to the 10.00 a.m., 1.20 p.m. and 5.45 p.m. down expresses. So, from their first winter of operation, the famous Anglo-Scottish express enjoyed A4 haulage.

Her drab 1950s appearance is in sharp contrast to when A3 No. 60043 *Brown Jack*, as LNER No. 2508, headed the inaugural 1936 down 'Flying Scotsman'. This unit was the last of the non-streamlined Gresley Pacifics to be built from scratch, completed in early 1935. (Photomatic)

The authoritative RCTS history of LNER locomotives (Vol. 2A), records that the new corridor tenders built for the four 'Silver' A4s, and seven of those constructed for the next (1936/7) batch, had only eight tons of coal capacity. This was because of additional plating being incorporated to enhance the streamlined effect of the overall design, and the loss of one ton's coal capacity was thought not to be a problem on a lightweight London–Newcastle service. However, the shortsightedness of this reduction was to become evident later, with the first-ever record of a through Edinburgh–London working running completely out of coal.

Meanwhile, with A1s and A3s supplying the power, the 'Non-Stop' had notched up more than 47,000 miles of non-stop running in the summer of 1935 with a total loss of only three minutes on schedule. Two late arrivals accounted for this, both of them caused by permanent way works.

An order for ten new A4s was placed in January 1936, although none were delivered until the following December, an unusually long gestation period for locomotives on the LNER, possibly explained by the fact that government financial assistance was enlisted to make their construction possible. Both *Silver Link* and one of her 'sisters', No. 2511 *Silver King*, were recorded on the winter version of the 'Flying Scotsman', but when July came round, the 'Non-Stop' began with traditional motive-power.

The last year when non-streamlined Pacifics held sway on the non-stop 'Flying Scotsman' was 1936, the service now accelerated by a further fifteen minutes. Both the early A1 and the latest of the A3 class were represented on the first of the trains departing on 6 July. The down service was headed by the last A3 to be built, No. 2508

Brown Jack, barely eighteen months old. She was to be an Edinburgh-based engine for all of her twenty-nine years; her crew on this occasion were not recorded. In contrast, the third Gresley Pacific to be constructed, some thirteen years previously, headed the London-bound train – none other than the old warhorse *Flying Scotsman* herself. Her use from the northern end on the opening day is interesting, the previous known example of this happening having been in 1930.

Lady Wedgwood, attended by her husband, the LNER Chief General Manager, as well as the newly-knighted Sir Nigel Gresley, saw off the northbound 'Scotsman' from King's Cross, while the up express had George Mills, Divisional General Manager, performing the ritual of shaking hands with the crews. These consisted of Driver Walker and Fireman Payne, with Messrs Barwick and Chablis as the southern crew.

The accelerated schedule made possible a fast trip from London to Aberdeen, the 'Scotsman' connecting with a 5.25 p.m. departure from Waverley, giving an arrival in the 'Granite City' before 8.30 p.m. Aberdeen made much of this first accelerated arrival, the locomotive on the northern run, No. 2563 *William Whitelaw* (the victor of the 1928 'race' with the Imperial Airways 'plane) being greeted by a municipal delegation when she came to a stop one minute early. Her lucky crew were immediately treated to 'a cake and wine banquet' at the Palace Hotel.

But the LNER was not the only company prepared to run streamlined trains in Britain. The LMS, emboldened by the new blood injected into its locomotive department by former Swindon man William Stanier, was also interested in linking London and Glasgow by high-speed express. To assess the practicality of a six-hour timing over the 401 miles between the cities, a special trial was arranged for 16 and 17 November 1936.

On Monday the 16th, 'Princess Royal' Pacific No. 6201 *Princess Elizabeth* ran non-stop from Euston to Glasgow (Central) in the unprecedented time of five hours fifty-three minutes and forty-two seconds. The average speed was 68.2 mph, maintained over this huge distance with a trailing load of seven vehicles (one a dynamometer car), of 225 tons tare. London–Glasgow had never been subject to any of the Anglo–Scottish races in 1888, 1895 or 1901, simply because the East Coast route was some forty miles longer, and such a timing had never been thought necessary, even if attainable.

The crew selected were from Crewe North, owing to their familiarity with the main line both north and south of that point. The work of Driver T.J. Clarke and firemen Fleet and Shaw was all the more impressive considering the hill-climbing that was involved – a total of some fifteen miles at an average of around 1 in 80. This included Beattock Bank, ten miles long, having to be climbed when the engine had already run 350 miles non-stop. And how it was climbed! The approach speed at the foot of the bank (which is prefaced by a brief adverse gradient of 1 in 200) was 80 mph, but 56 mph was still being attained by the summit, the notorious incline being conquered in the unbelievable time of $9\frac{1}{2}$ minutes. No wonder the toast at Glasgow's Central Hotel, at a social function following the run, was 'Tom Clarke and his mates'.

The following day saw *Princess Elizabeth* running non-stop back to Euston with an extra coach (total gross weight 260 tons) at an average speed of exactly 70 mph, in five hours forty-four minutes and twenty seconds. It was a magnificent achievement, showing that there was an ample margin for a six hour timing between the cities, with a five minute stop for a crew change.

O.S. Nock writes in his book *Speed Records on Britain's Railways* that the LMS officer

One of the most famous protagonists of the non-stop story, Class 8P Pacific No. 46201 *Princess Elizabeth*, is seen climbing Beattock bank with a Birmingham–Glasgow express in the late 1950s. Her non-stop return journeys between London and Glasgow in November 1936 – the second of them made at an average speed of 70 mph – set a British record which lasted twelve years. This locomotive, like *Mallard*, is thankfully preserved. (D.A. Anderson)

responsible for the organizing of the runs, R.A. Riddles (later the leader of the design team which produced BR's Standard locomotives), had the most trying time in ensuring their success. Apparently, a defect was only detected in *Princess Elizabeth* on the Sunday afternoon before the test and Riddles, assistant to the CME William Stanier (then absent in India), ordered that a spare part be brought from Crewe works. This involved a senior member of the company's staff rummaging through the darkened spare parts department of the closed works by the light of a match! Success was achieved through the help of a roused storekeeper, the vital part being sent to London by the last afternoon train. Riddles stayed up all night preparing the engine, but if he anticipated making up for it with a sound sleep in Glasgow on the Monday night, he was much mistaken. The Pacific had to be moved to St Rollox for piston re-metalling overnight, a task that was completed only just in time. Such is the spirit required of record-breakers.

The *Railway Gazette* enthused, 'With little doubt these runs are the fastest that have ever been made in the world by steam power over a non-stop distance greater than 300 miles,' although the magazine went on to point out that the LNER's *Silver Link* had averaged 70 mph for 465 miles a day (i.e. King's Cross–Darlington and back) for nearly three weeks on the earliest runs of the 'Silver Jubilee'. Nevertheless, no one would contest the significance of the LMS's achievement. All the more of a pity that the resulting London–Glasgow streamliner, the 'Coronation Scot', had a more relaxed 6½-hour schedule.

Incidentally, it seems extraordinary in retrospect that the LMS did not equip its new Pacifics with corridor tenders. One was built by the LMS for test purposes in 1937, its construction begun at Crewe and finished at Derby, but there is little reference to this in the contemporary technical literature and it was converted back to a normal arrangement around 1950, running for most of its life coupled to a 'Black Five' 4–6–0 (No. 45235 when scrapped around 1966).

But while the LNER was ordering more A4s, and the LMS breaking all records between Euston and Glasgow, diesel power was once again putting *Silver Link* and *Princess Elizabeth* into perspective. On 23 October 1936, a second generation of diesel railcar on the CB and Q Railroad travelled non-stop 1,017.2 miles between Chicago and Denver in twelve hours twelve minutes and thirty-seven seconds. The average speed over the distance – in the opposite direction to the run nearly 2½ years earlier – was approximately 84 mph, with a maximum of 116 mph. A total of 120 passengers rode in the two power plus six trailing car rake of the 'Denver Zephyr'. The 465 tons gross load was powered by no less than 3,000 bhp in the two power units, consuming over 1,300 gallons of fuel.

Whether the 3,000-odd army of crossing-keepers was required once more was not recorded by the technical press, nor was there any explanation of the two-mile addition to the overall distance travelled, although this southbound journey appears to have been via Oreapolis rather than by Omaha, as two years earlier. The train started from Chicago's Union Station (at 7 a.m. Central time) creating a new non-stop record by arriving at Denver at 6.12 p.m. Mountain Time.

It stands as a world record for non-stop rail travel to this day.

If 1936 saw LNER admirers becoming used to the comings and goings of the 'Silver Jubilee', with its locomotives of unprecedented appearance, the following year included the introduction of two more streamlined expresses on the East Coast main line. The more important of these, as far as our story is concerned, was the 'Coronation', a comparatively heavy (312 ton), blue-liveried express scheduled to bring London and Edinburgh together in six hours. Both up and down trains would leave the respective capitals in late afternoon, at 4 p.m. (down) and 4.30 p.m. (up), something not possible prior to 1932 when such departure times would give arrivals well past midnight. Supplied with its own 'marque' of five A4 Pacifics, all of them named after the major Commonwealth dominions, the 'Coronation' made its debut at King's Cross on 5 July 1937.

No. 4491 *Commonwealth of Australia* was at the head of the new northbound streamliner, the newly-named No. 4489 *Dominion of Canada* powering the up train, with Driver Binnie marking his sixty-fourth birthday at the controls. Scenes reminiscent of 1928 were witnessed at King's Cross. No fewer than 2,000 people are believed to have seen off the first down 'Coronation', whose progress past Wood Green was televised by the BBC. Edinburgh was reached one minute early by *Commonwealth of Australia* working right through with a stop at York (a Newcastle stop was later added without an increase in overall journey time).

But these were not the only A4s making the headlines that 5 July, for the 'Flying Scotsman' was being accelerated yet again, this time down to seven hours exactly. No. 4484 *Falcon* headed the first down train, according to the *LNER Magazine*, her crew and all details of the first up working not being recorded, although another source has No. 4482 *Golden Eagle* operating from King's Cross and No. 4485 *Kestrel* from Edinburgh. This day marked the beginning of A4 haulage of the non-stop Anglo–Scottish services that was to last into the decade of Man's first visit to the Moon.

So busy was the northbound 'Scotsman' on Saturday 31 July that the express was followed by no fewer than three relief trains. Normally, the 'Non-Stop' loaded to twelve coaches, with two extra being taken on Saturdays. Given the 420-minute schedule, the 'Scotsman' was no easy operating matter, prompting C.J. Allen to observe later: 'This famous train had now become one of the most formidable propositions of locomotive haulage in Great Britain, especially south of York'.

Final running and punctuality figures do not appear to have been recorded for the first year of almost exclusively A4 haulage. We know that No. 4492 *Dominion of New Zealand*, temporarily allocated to Haymarket, notched up no fewer than fifty-two consecutive trips (practically 50 per cent) on the non-stop 'Scotsman' without a break, totalling 20,436 miles, but the non-streamlined Pacifics were not entirely out of the picture, with the much-vaunted No. 2750 *Papyrus* making one last return working, down to Edinburgh on 6 August and working up again the next day. The following month her corridor tender was transferred to an A4; no A1 or A3 was now so equipped. Needless to say, on the principle that you can't keep a good locomotive down, at least one through Edinburgh–London journey was to be achieved by one of the former class in 1938 on the 'Coronation', even with a eight-ton coal supply.

Surprisingly, the earliest A4s also carried no more than eight tons of coal when working throughout the 393 miles on the 'Coronation' services, although this was considered sufficient capacity; the whole point of streamlining was not only to facilitate high speed, but to make such speeds easier to sustain with a reduced fuel consumption. That was the theory anyway, but this was the first time that locomotives, streamlined or not, had been rostered to operate between the capitals throughout the winter. On 2

A4 No. 4498 *Sir Nigel Gresley* nears Ganwick with the up 'Flying Scotsman' in 1938. As no precise date is available for this picture, it must be conjectured that a passenger vehicle has been added immediately behind the tender before departure from Waverley, or this is the train during the non-summer timetable. (Photomatic)

December 1937 No. 4490 *Empire of India* disgraced itself on the up 'Coronation' by having to stop at Hitchin, its tender bereft of coal. Obviously, headwinds could play havoc with coal consumption figures in the winter months, and northern crews had already experienced difficulties on down journeys. The Hitchin incident was sufficiently serious to prompt the immediate decision to modify the new corridor tenders. Nine tons of coal would now be carried after the removal of the streamlined fairing at the front of the tenders. Those 1928 tenders originally fitted to un-streamlined Pacifics and now running with A4s soon had to undergo their second modification within a short time to restore their original nine-ton capacity.

The 1937–8 winter saw a twenty-minute relaxation in the schedule of the 'Flying Scotsman', stopping at Grantham, York, Newcastle and Berwick in each direction, plus Darlington on the up journey. But from 4 July, it was back to a seven-hour non-stop timing – and for seven days a week. Sunday 10 July 1938 thus saw the creation of another minor record – the first non-stop Anglo–Scottish journey on the Sabbath. The previous Sunday had seen a record created of rather greater importance, for on 3 July the new double-chimney A4 No. 4468 *Mallard* set a new world speed record for steam traction of 126 mph in descending Stoke Bank, between Grantham and Peterborough. *Mallard*'s achievement has passed into railway lore; the fact that she also currently holds the world record for non-stop steam operation seems less well-known – but more of that later.

The 1938 non-stop programme was launched on 4 July, with most of the attention being paid to the rolling stock. This was the fifth generation of new stock for the train,

An A4 is in charge of the train for the start of the 1939 summer timetable. No. 4482 *Golden Eagle* is seen leaving the London terminus at the beginning of its 393-mile run. (Hulton Picture Company)

No. 4492 *Dominion of New Zealand* leaves a smoke-screen across the sky as it heads the 'Flying Scotsman' service. The engine is in its original form with valancing partly covering the coupled wheels, the latest fashion during the 1930s, although decidedly dated in appearance today. This valance was later removed from the engines in the class to facilitate maintenance and increase the air flow to the centre big end. (R.A. Collection)

setting new standards in sound insulation, with double-glazed windows and cushioned flooring. This was in addition to the renewed standards of comfort and convenience in other aspects of travel, including a buffet facility to supplement the usual restaurant car provision.

No details appear to have been recorded of the first down journey, but there was a modest ceremony at Edinburgh to celebrate the first up departure. Director Andrew K. McCosh, accompanied by Gresley, was pictured inspecting the preserved Great Northern 'Single' No. 1 standing at Waverley's Platform 2 (now vanished), her streamlined successor in the background. Although we know that the up train was headed by No. 4489 *Dominion of Canada*, other details, including the overall season's punctuality figures, were not publicized in the LNER's house magazine. It was reported elsewhere that the 'Non-Stop' usually loaded to thirteen coaches during the summer and that timekeeping was good, except on Saturdays. The 105 miles from Grantham to King's Cross had to be covered at exactly a mile a minute, this with what could be anything up to 550 tons on a non-stop journey already nearly 300 miles long.

The 1939 'Non-Stop' season began on 3 July with no report from King's Cross; Waverley at least produced one photographer to record Divisional General Manager George Mills waving off the train, hauled by No. 4484 *Kingfisher*, appropriately painted in blue. Her crews were Driver Snare and Fireman Roy of Gateshead, and Driver Ardinan and Fireman King of King's Cross.

The LNER's Publicity Department issued a press release for the newspapers itemizing the number of non-stop runs over the London–Edinburgh stretch in the summers 1928–38. This came to 702 journeys in each direction, a total mileage of more than half a million, achieved with a high record of punctuality on a schedule which was certainly too lax to begin with but tightened up considerably, and with no relaxation in train weight.

War was expected soon, and the LNER was not going to be taken by surprise. The three streamlined services on the East Coast route were terminated after 31 August, some forty-eight hours in advance of the declaration. Indeed, a number of A4 locomotives were actually put into store. There was a general feeling, fuelled by an inflated interpretation of the Luftwaffe's strength, that bombing of British cities would begin immediately. Not only did this mean that all four railway companies had to immediately improvise evacuation specials for urban children, but the LNER put some its most powerful passenger locomotives into mothballs when its motive power requirements were greatest.

Compared with the First World War, there was an immediate contraction of public passenger services. While most express trains maintained their status, schedules, even their restaurant cars, for some 3½ years from 1914, the Second World War opened very differently for the LNER. 'Full emergency working' was the rule from 9 September, six days into the war, with only basic services and no catering *en route*, although a less spartan timetable prevailed from the twenty-fifth of the month, with restaurant cars returning by mid-October. Nevertheless, the 'Flying Scotsman' flew no longer. Nine hours and twenty-five minutes was now required for the journey between the capitals, with lengthy station stops (fifteen minutes at Grantham) to permit passengers to purchase comestibles.

By October the LNER had lost no less than 25 per cent of its passenger business, balanced by a 20 per cent increase in freight tonnage. If the 1935–9 period had been the

The original black and silver livery of certain members of the A4 class is shown to advantage in this view of No. 4493 *Peregrine* – later re-named *Lord Faringdon*. Unfortunately the colour scheme tended to discolour quickly in service while the joints in the streamlined casing became collecting points for the grime inseparable from the steam engine. Notice in the background the Great Northern somersault signals. (R.A. Collection)

'Age of the Passenger', with East and West Coast streamliners joining and surpassing the non-stop 'Flying Scotsman', 1939–45 was the period when the traveller would be asked, 'Is your journey really necessary?'

The war brought to an end Gateshead's involvement in non-stop running. Tyneside crews had made a major contribution to the success of the 'Flying Scotsman's' operations, forming a majority of those initially involved in what was in engineering, if not outright commercial, terms, an outstanding success. Their record was all the more creditable when their necessarily convoluted four-day diagrams are borne in mind.

The 'Non-Stop' story on Britain's pre-Second World War railways was as much a human as an engineering achievement. The LMS crews who could travel over 300 miles without catering or sanitary facilities and still reach their destination 'as fit as fiddles', the Gateshead men who were separated from their families for three full days (in which they crewed locomotives for only fourteen hours), all made a massive contribution to express railway services in this country. Such dedication was fortunately not required again of them in the more enlightened days after 1945. Indeed, the whole 'Non-Stop' saga was brought to a halt which was to last nearly a whole decade.

The Year of the Rain

Nineteen forty-eight was the year of the rain. Not only was the first northbound 'Flying Scotsman' waved on its non-stop journey in teeming rain by the Lord Mayor of London, but rain was to play a major role that year in the smashing of the world non-stop record for steam traction.

With worn-out staff and *matériel*, the railways took an understandably long time to recover from the effects of six gruelling years of total war. In May 1946, the LNER had used A4 No. 2512 *Silver Fox* on a six-coach test run between London and Edinburgh in 378½ minutes, mainly to assess maximum speed limits in immediate post-war track conditions. Despite 102 mph being attained on the return journey near Essendine, there was no resulting speeding up of Anglo–Scottish express services, and no lightweight high-speed fliers at all. Another two years were to pass before Britain's railways, nationalized from the first day of 1948, could make a brave gesture to hark back to the glamorous inter-war years of the 'Flying Scotsman'.

King's Cross station, Monday 31 May 1948. The non-stop 'Flying Scotsman' recommenced its summer programme – it was to be its last summer – with newly renumbered No.60034 *Lord Faringdon* setting off with the down train, and Haymarket's No. 60009 *Union of South Africa* heading the up, with Driver Bell at the regulator. The latter engine had also powered the last up 'Coronation' before the commencement of war nine years previously. The 'Scotsman' had a disappointing timing ten minutes short of eight hours. Admittedly, there was an official 90 mph ceiling in force on the East Coast main line, restricting the train's ability to recover any lost time.

A buffet car was added to the flush-sided rake, which also included the 'Silver Princess' coach, an American-built vehicle with aircraft-type seating and lighting. It was sponsored by Pressed Steel Ltd., and described by the late Brian Haresnape as 'a promising attempt to improve on the typical British steel-panelled coach . . . definitely a missed opportunity'.

The first up journey seems to have been fairly eventful, with an aviation accident delaying the train in Northumberland and a stop having to be made for water at Grantham owing to damage inflicted on the water-scoop, possibly because of 'dipping' at too high a speed at Muskham troughs in an effort to recover lost time. This latter point is pure speculation, but the up 'Scotsman' was recorded as passing Wood Green at nine

minutes past six, already some twenty-five minutes late. For most of 1948's early non-stop trips, King's Cross rostered Nos. 60033/4, with Nos. 60004/9/12 appearing from the northern end. *Lord Faringdon* (previously known as *Peregrine*) ran hot on her second down trip, being replaced by No. 60004 *William Whitelaw*, which continued on the service until the King's Cross engine was fit to resume on 11 June. For a while Haymarket engines thus monopolized the re-introduced 'Non-Stop', although No. 60009 had another interrupted journey on 2 June, having to stop at Newcastle for the removal of a sick passenger. Another untoward incident occurred on 15 July, when the corridor tender connection jammed between No. 60033 *Seagull* and the train. A stop was made at Pilmoor for the crews to change over.

All these incidents pale into insignificance compared to what afflicted the 'Flying Scotsman' on the not-so-glorious 12 August of that year. It is worth looking at this extraordinary, and still unexplained, event, to understand the background to one of the most important achievements in the realms of British passenger train operations.

Rainfall had already been heavy in the Scottish Borders in the first week of August, but on Thursday the twelfth, phenomenal weather conditions occurred. Four hundred million tons of water fell on the Tweed Valley in a twenty-four hour period, the equivalent of 6 in of rainfall over an extraordinarily wide area. Streams and rivers were turned into torrents, the Tweed itself – which was already in spate three days earlier – over-reaching its previous highwater record of 1831 by some $3\frac{1}{2}$ ft at Kelso.

The railways through the area were immediately inundated. The East Coast main line was cut in thirteen places, with seven bridges being swept away between Grantshouse and Reston, and six landslides occurring. Near Ayton a rail embankment acted as a dam for floodwater, the new lake being some five miles long, 300 yards wide, and up to 40 ft deep in places. If the embankment gave way, the coastal town of Eyemouth, whose branch line was cut when a viaduct pier fell down, would be in considerable danger, and coastguards had to stand twenty-four hour watches ready to fire warning rockets over the town. The Tweed Valley line from Tweedmouth to St. Boswells was blocked by a landslip near the Anglo-Scottish Border at Carham, and almost all the border branches had to close, in the case of the Jedburgh and St. Boswells–Duns lines, permanently, as far as passenger services were concerned. On the Waverley Route there were four landslides and Galashiels station was flooded.

The town of Berwick-on-Tweed awoke the next day to find itself completely cut off from the outside world. The East Coast line, as well as being blocked to the north where Grantshouse and Burnmouth stations were flooded, had blockages to the south at Chathill and Goswick. Berwick signal box was inoperable and the station closed. The town's main roads to north and south were impassable and four long-distance London–Edinburgh buses were marooned in the town, along with twenty-two coachloads of day trippers from Tyneside who had to spend the night in a garage. Berwick's weather forecast for the day had been 'local showers'!

A number of trains had been caught in this meteorological holocaust. A passenger train was stranded overnight on one of the Berwickshire branches, and three freights were to be marooned for days on the East Coast main line. Three express passenger trains had been heading north as the worst effects of the weather began to be felt. The 09.50 a.m., 10.00 a.m. and 10.05 a.m., all ex-King's Cross, were all full, at what was supposed to be the height of the English holiday season. The middle train in this

bedraggled procession was of course the non-stop 'Flying Scotsman', and it managed as far north as Alnmouth before being sent back to Newcastle. This put it behind its relief, the 10.05, which had already been pathed westwards from Newcastle to Carlisle and over the Waverley Route to Edinburgh. Meanwhile, the 09.50 had managed to struggle through to the Scottish capital by the Tweedmouth–St. Boswells line and the northern part of the Waverley Route, some 200 minutes late.

When the newspapers went to press in the early hours of Friday 13 August, the 10.05 ex-King's Cross was stuck at Tynehead, only sixteen miles from Edinburgh on the Waverley Route, with food being taken by road to the 500 stranded passengers, while of the 'Flying Scotsman', one of the world's most famous trains, there was no news at all.

If these natural disasters seem to have no place in the story of non-stop railway express operations, it is precisely *because* of these natural conditions that the longest non-stop journeys in British railway history occurred. Indeed, rail controllers in the border areas deserved all possible credit for preventing any loss of life by adopting a 'safety first' policy throughout the crisis. Just how seriously one train was threatened is best illustrated in O.S. Nock's account of a phone-call from the driver of the 10.05 at Tynehead to inform Edinburgh Control that the train could proceed no further. When asked, 'Why not?', the weary driver, believed to have been Haymarket's Bill Nairn, replied that he was already up to his waist in water!

The passengers from this marooned express were ferried to Edinburgh by road the next morning, a famished goat being ferried in the train's guard's van promptly eating much of the upholstery in the replacement bus!

Meanwhile, the 'Flying Scotsman' had managed to reach the Scottish capital after yet another detour. After travelling from Newcastle to Carlisle, the train penetrated as far as Hawick on the Waverley Route before having to retrace its steps for the second time, and attempt the former West Coast main line to Strawfrank junction, near Carstairs, and then proceed to Edinburgh. Even in the city there was a diversion. Instead of proceeding to the logical terminus of Princes Street station, the train reversed from Dalry Road down to the former North British system at Haymarket West junction, whence Waverley was reached at nine minutes to four in the morning. It is believed to have been the worst-ever journey made by the famous train in peacetime. There may have been an even more calamitous one featuring the 'Scotsman' in a wartime snowstorm, but it has no place in this story.

'It may be years before the bridges can be rebuilt', a BR official was quoted as commenting when the great tidy-up began. All Edinburgh–London expresses were immediately diverted via Carstairs, the up 'Flying Scotsman' now starting westwards from Waverley and making its first stop within two miles, to attach a pilot at the rear of the train at Haymarket West for the climb to Dalry Road on the former Caledonian system. From here the A4 was pointing in the correct direction, and, stopping for water where necessary, London was reached anything up to twelve hours later.

It was soon found that this enormous (almost 50 per cent) addition to the journey time could be reduced by bypassing the entire East Coast route between Shaftesholme junction, just north of Doncaster, diverting the 'Scotsman' over the Settle and Carlisle line. For railway enthusiasts it must have seemed a unique opportunity – to travel between London and Edinburgh over part of all three of the pre-grouping Anglo–Scottish routes, and with the same A4 all the way! Former LNER Pacifics were to

A4 No. 60031 *Golden Plover* breasts Falahill summit, 880 ft above sea level, with the northbound 'Flying Scotsman' during the Border floods emergency of 1948. Although this unique photograph records a diversion which was negotiated seventeen times for a new world steam non-stop record of 408.65 miles, it is not believed to show one of the record attempts. (John Robertson)

become regular performers over the Settle–Carlisle line just before dieselization in 1961, but this was a novel sight at the time. Indeed, on one occasion the down 'Scotsman' was headed north from Leeds by a 'Black Five' 4–6–0, No. 45223 piloted by 2P 4–4–0, No. 40459, presumably because of engine failure.

This might have seemed the logical route for the non-stop 'Flying Scotsman' to take between the capitals, but other East Coast expresses needed to be re-routed via Newcastle for Tyneside business, and with the end of the summer timetable not too far in the future, when the 'Scotsman' would revert to its stopping pattern, all possible efforts were made to re-direct all services to the east of the country. From 16 August the Waverley Route and Tweed Valley lines were passable, with some single-line working, but in the up direction only. The 7.50 p.m. ex-Waverley was the first express to use this route, while that day's up 'Scotsman' travelled the entire Waverley Route to Carlisle. By the seventeenth it was decided to re-route all express traffic via Galashiels and Kelso, with an emergency timetable formalizing this from Monday 23 August.

One which didn't get through non-stop! Blue-liveried A4 No. 60031 *Golden Plover* takes water at Tweedmouth while working an unidentified East Coast express southwards during the floods emergency of 1948. The loco's crew could hardly be blamed for taking water at a column when the diversionary route included a bank as severe as Falahill and a single-line stretch with a 25 mph speed restriction. (W.E. Boyd collection)

From this date, all northbound East Coast express passenger trains would travel the East Coast main line as far as Tweedmouth, just south of Berwick-on-Tweed. The Tweed Valley line was then followed westwards; this was a North Eastern Railway branch from Tweedmouth which made an end-on junction with the North British at Kelso, the actual border being east of this point, at Carham. This line, single for most of the former NBR section, brought the traffic to a junction just south of St. Boswells on the Carlisle–Edinburgh Waverley Route. From this point, Edinburgh was only forty-five miles to the north, although there was an enormous obstacle to be overcome – Falahill. This was a 900 ft summit reached by some $9\frac{1}{2}$ miles of around 1 in 70 from the north, and by longer, but more moderate, adverse gradients from the south. Despite its main-line status, the Waverley Route's curves denied any opportunity of making up lost time by high speeds. Not that speeds were foremost in the minds of footplatemen at that time – just getting to the destination was enough.

With an extra ninety minutes added officially to the 'Flying Scotsman's' timing, the 'Non-Stop' was expected to make stops for water as required at Tweedmouth and Galashiels. Banking assistance was available for up trains at Hardengreen, at the foot of the climb to Falahill. From these unpromising circumstances were to come the longest non-stop runs in British railway history, and longest authenticated runs by steam power anywhere in the world.

Compared with the ballyhoo which greeted the opening of the first non-stop service between London and Edinburgh, and the efforts which the LMS made to surpass it, the breaking of the long-distance non-stop record on British railway tracks is shrouded in obscurity.

Before the end of 1948, the *BR Magazine* reported that 'on certain occasions' the 'Flying Scotsman' had extended its non-stop run to 408½ miles by negotiating the enforced diversion without stopping for water. The magazine went on to say, 'On many of these occasions the trains arrived at their destinations on time, and the conditions of the engines and the reserve of coal and oil available were such that a further journey of 80 to 100 miles could easily have been undertaken'.

This low-key description is echoed in the manner of the record's announcement in the *Railway Magazine* for March/April 1949, where Cecil J. Allen announced, 'My first business is to raise my hat to Driver Swan, of Haymarket shed . . . for his share in a very notable achievement'. Yet contemporary sources suggest that Driver Jimmy Swan was not the first to set up the record of 408.65 miles, this honour falling to his colleague Bill Stevenson.

The records show that, on 24 August, this driver decided to eschew banking assistance over Falahill by running as hard as possible through Hardengreen (no easy matter given the previous Eskbank curves). On the bank itself there were sufficient freights looped to provide emergency banking assistance in the event of a stall, the climb being accomplished with 35 per cent cut-off, according to Norman McKillop's account in his 1958 book *Enginemen Elite*. (The late Mr McKillop also credited the first such run to Driver Swan.) Probably more difficult for the engine crew was the necessarily sedate pace on the western part of the Tweed Valley line, with its 25 mph speed restriction for Pacifics, the tender's water-level lowering all the time.

In the better-documented run by Swan on 7 September, the A4 (No. 60029 *Woodcock* on both occasions) still had some 2,000 gallons available by the time Lucker troughs were reached, and a further 2,500 picked up there. C.J. Allen believed that this amount, some 500 gallons short of full capacity, would still create problems for the crew, with nearly 100 miles to go to the next set of troughs at Wiske Moor. A full pick-up would be essential at the North Yorkshire troughs to ensure no problems over the next seventy-four miles to Scrooby, with the southern crew in charge by this time. Allen's information appears to have come from Mr Ronald Nelson, and he concludes, again writing exclusively about Driver Swan's achievements: 'There is reason to believe that on most, if not all, of the days concerned, the train was not actually brought to a stand . . . on the York–King's Cross stage'.

This underlines the importance of remembering that it was not only Haymarket drivers who set up the new non-stop record for British, indeed European, rail operations, but was very much a team effort involving the King's Cross crews. Traditionally, they had to deal with the more tightly-timed section of the runs, but on northbound journeys would have to husband the locomotive and its fuel resources to meet the demands of the longer-than-normal route and the greater time duration.

The six A4s which were driven non-stop (as far as we know) are listed in the Appendix on p. 113, along with their drivers. It must be stressed that this record of 408.65 miles non-stop, an undoubted British and European record, and almost certainly a world record for steam power, given the obscure nature of the 1876 run on the Pennsylvania Railroad, was neither officially ordered nor sanctioned by railway management.

It was the result of careful but imaginative locomotive operation, the product of four men working as a team with a machine far more unpredictable and labour-intensive than the diesels which had set records on the other side of the Atlantic. It was almost a gesture of railway operation at its grassroots best; a triumph of improvisation over the oldest elements of all.

Freight rolled again on the Scottish section of the East Coast mainline by the end of October 1948, and the 'Flying Scotsman' was able to return to the route by 1 November. By this time, the train was back in its winter stopping configuration; one which, in effect, it was never to leave.

Steam's Indian summer on the East Coast route

A new non-stop service between London and Edinburgh was introduced in 1949; it was also the year of the longest diesel non-stop run in British rail history.

But to King's Cross, 23 May 1949, where steam still reigned supreme. Actress Anne Crawford cut a red, white and blue ribbon ranged in front of A4 No. 60010 *Dominion of Canada* to launch the first new Anglo–Scottish express since the war. The A4's headboard bore the words 'The Capitals Limited'; the 'Flying Scotsman' had lost its non-stop accolade to this newcomer.

Many rail writers had speculated for years on the desirability or otherwise of giving the traditional 'Scotsman' a dichotomous image; non-stop in the summer, but a catch-all 'omnibus' express in the winter months. The publicity value of the non-stop achievement was somewhat dissipated by applying it to a train which was well enough known already, and some critics felt that an entirely different express should have been introduced much earlier, using the 'Non-Stop' banner to attract maximum publicity.

Be that as it may, the 'Capitals Limited' took its bow in 1949, leaving King's Cross at 9.30 each summer morning with exclusively air-conditioned stock. The earlier departure time was supposedly intended to improve early evening connections northwards from Edinburgh, although any such advantage only applied to the down train. In the case of the up service, leaving Waverley at 9.45 a.m., the new express obviously afforded poorer connections from northern centres; in particular a departure was necessary from Aberdeen at five minutes to six in the morning. Haymarket stalwart No. 60027 *Merlin* powered the first southbound train.

As it was, the 'Capitals Limited' had an eight-hour schedule between the cities of its title; shades of the bad old 1896 agreement! Possibly there was an excuse for this poor timing, owing to speed restrictions (some as low as 5 mph) on the newly re-opened Berwick–Dunbar section, and there was to be an admirable acceleration programme put into effect over the next five years. At the time of its introduction, the new 'Limited' reached Edinburgh at 17.30, giving eventual arrivals at Dundee at 19.22 and Aberdeen at 21.20. The 'Flying Scotsman', remaining at its old ten o'clock starting time, now made three stops in a ponderous eight hour twenty-eight minute schedule.

The streamlined A4s were still the undisputed motive-power for the non-stop services crossing the border, despite the introduction of newer Pacifics from the drawing-boards of Gresley's successors, Thompson and Peppercorn. In particular, the latter's A1 Pacifics

Sporting an early BR livery with full wording on the tender, No. 60027 *Merlin* passes Doncaster on the up 'Capitals Limited' in June 1949. (J. Davenport)

Despite being to a design introduced some years after the A4s, the A1 Pacifics of 1945 were never rostered for the non-stop services although they did work a number of the other prestige ER passenger trains. Nos. 60147 *North Eastern* and 60126 *Sir Vincent Raven* are seen within the roundhouse at York in the company of two Class 9 2–10–0s. (Courtney Haydon)

(not to be confused with LNER No. 4472 and her sisters, now entirely re-classified as A3), were powerful machines which soon came to be respected by East Coast railwaymen, if not exactly taken to their hearts.

Some railway historians have employed valuable printer's ink in speculating why the new A1s did not provide motive-power for the 'Capitals Limited' from its inception in 1949. P.N. Townend believes that the answer lay in the fact that the new engines had steam-braked tenders, while the existing corridor tenders were vacuum-braked. This would not appear to have been an insuperable technical obstacle if railway management had been determined that the A1s should succeed the Gresley engines on the 'Non-Stop', and F.A.S. Brown goes even farther down this speculative dead-end. In his biography of Sir Nigel Gresley, Brown recounts that there was much railway gossip at the time of the A1s' introduction that the inheritors of Gresley's patents would not allow the construction of new corridor tenders for the A1s, something Brown believed could have been circumvented by simply using existing corridor tenders. In fact, since there is no evidence that the corridor tender was ever patented by Gresley in the UK in the first place, such baroque speculation is surely unnecessary.

O.S. Nock is probably nearer the mark in suggesting that the larger firebox with a 50 sq ft grate area of the A1 meant that this newer class of locomotives were heavier coal burners on trains requiring a medium power output. Cecil J. Allen believed in 1951 that an A1 would have to be driven at 5 per cent longer cut-off than an A4, with a possibly critical resulting increase in coal consumption. However, these facts might not have been realised so soon in the A1's career and it is entirely possible that the locomotive authorities on the former LNER main line simply decided to leave well alone, as far as the unique non-stop service was concerned. In any event, with the A4s having set up a new world non-stop record for steam traction on seventeen occasions the previous year, what possible need could there be for a change to a new and comparatively untried unit?

Even newer and more untried than the latest Pacifics on the East Coast main line was an innovation on the West Coast – the introduction into traffic in 1949 of a pair of 1,600 bhp diesel-electric locomotives, Nos. 10000 and 10001. Designed by H.G. Ivatt, the LMS's last CME, and built by English Electric, the new units were intended to offer comparisons with existing express steam locomotives. Whether this was an entirely fair comparison, given that the LMS had produced no postwar steam designs in this particular power category, is a moot point. Certainly, the twin diesels were to operate alongside the 'Coronation' class Pacifics and, impressive though these latter machines were, it is entirely possible that their real potential was never realized, owing to the failure to provide mechanized stoking equipment to feed the class's massive fireboxes.

But our story concerns non-stop running, and Nos 10000/1 were to add an interesting passage to this by becoming only the third locomotive, or more correctly locomotive unit, to run non-stop northwards from London (Euston) to Glasgow (Central), a distance about a mile over the 400 mark.

This they did on 1 June 1949, on a special demonstration run on the down 'Royal Scot', comprising sixteen coaches of about 545 tons gross. Two coaches contained special parties from BR and the English Electric Company, the former including such illustrious post-war engineers as Ivatt himself and R.A. Riddles, who was later largely responsible for the BR standard locomotives.

In teeming rain, the pair of diesels set off for Glasgow, showing their mettle in the very first mile. The climb to Camden No. 1 Box was accomplished in $2\frac{1}{2}$ minutes, a timing unknown to steam-power with this scale of load. Point-to-point times were easily reached, so much so that the diesels had to be eased to avoid running too far ahead of time, and with a maximum speed of only $73\frac{1}{2}$ mph. Hampered by a slothful eight hours twenty-five minutes schedule for the run, Nos.10000/1 had really no opportunity to show their paces except in hill-climbing, rivalling the unprecedented times achieved by 'Coronation' No. 6234 *Duchess of Abercorn* in February 1939 with a slightly heavier load when on a Crewe–Glasgow test run. Bearing in mind that the diesels' hill-climbing ability could be acquired by simply moving the control lever, the steam engine's comparative times can only be marvelled at, achieved as they were by the product of human toil. As it was, the diesels effortlessly bettered the passing timings of the 1939 'Royal Scot' when it was on a seven-hour schedule but with a 100 ton lesser load.

The technical press recorded that the Glasgow arrival time was three minutes early, but failed to mention if any special crewing arrangements had been made. One observer commented that the gangway doors between the units had been open for the journey, suggesting that a replacement driver or crew may have sat in the rear-most cab when not on duty, but the accounts do not mention if there was a corresponding open gangway into the train itself. There was no technical reason why there could not be (as library copies of the driver's manual make clear), but it does appear that an opportunity was hereby lost to assess the prospects of a truly non-stop 'Royal Scot' service between London and Glasgow on a regular basis. Certainly from 10 July that year the famous express was

Four months after their non-stop run between Euston and Glasgow (Central) on the 'Royal Scot', LMS diesels Nos. 10000/1 are seen heading the up train through Tebay in October 1949. (Photomatic)

A perennial performer on the 'Non-Stop' roster, A4 No. 60009 *Union of South Africa* is seen near Croft Spa on the down 'Capitals Limited' in June 1950. Eleven years later this engine headed the last 'Non-Stop' in the up direction. (Photomatic)

A monochrome print cannot do full justice to this view of A4 No. 60003 *Andrew K. McCosh* in BR blue livery as it powers the up 'Capitals Limited' south of Darlington in June 1950. (Photomatic)

In August 1952, its last year of operation before being re-named, the down 'Capitals Limited' is seen at speed near Darlington behind Haymarket A4 No. 60004 *William Whitelaw*. (Photomatic)

advertised as running non-stop between the cities, while actually stopping for crew changing at Carlisle (Kingmoor) shed, as in the late 1920s. If nothing else, Nos. 10000/1 achieved the longest non-stop diesel-hauled run in British railway history, one which has still not been excelled in the years of progressive dieselization which followed 1955. These forgotten pioneer diesels may also have hauled the heaviest non-stop train over 400 miles on British metals.

Interestingly, while the 'Royal Scot' featured prominently in the list of long-distance express journeys achieved in 1949, along with of course the 'Capitals Limited', there were two Western Region runs upholding former GWR traditions. These were the (Saturdays only) 10.30 Paddington–Truro, and 10.35 Paddington–Plymouth, covering $279\frac{1}{4}$ and $225\frac{3}{4}$ miles respectively without a stop. The periodical press in 1950 also carried an intriguing reference to a 'one off' through locomotive working between London and Perth by 'Coronation' class Pacific No. 46224 *Princess Alexandra* with a sixteen-coach

load on the 19.20 ex-Euston. Although not non-stop, this 450-mile run must rank as one of the longest through engine workings in British rail history, and a searching test of locomotive endurance.

More puzzling, however, is the comparative absence of punctuality statistics – indeed very much publicity at all – about the non-stop service between London and Edinburgh. No longer were summaries of the summer's running being published in the periodical press and, given the doubtful commercial value of a service omitting all intermediate stops, the whole *raison d'être* of the 'Capitals Limited' was undermined. There was no point in cutting out obvious stops at, say, York and Newcastle, which even the 'Coronation' express had honoured, unless it brought in resulting publicity. Certainly, radio personality Derek McCulloch ('Uncle Mac') made a 1949 journey on the train, including the footplate of No. 60033, although his broadcast on 1 August that year was obviously aimed at children.

Whether in the limelight or not, Gresley's A4s carried on their own high traditions into 1950 on the 'Non-Stop'. No. 60009 *Union of South Africa* operated the service for 4½ weeks continuously that year, including balancing Sunday workings, bettered only by her Haymarket sister No. 60031 *Golden Plover* which ran forty trips in 5½ weeks in July and August.

As for performance, record-breaking Bill Stevenson is recorded that summer as having run the approximate sixty miles between Tweedmouth and Edinburgh in 52 minutes on his beloved A4 No. 60027 *Merlin* on a down 'Capitals Limited' service which had been delayed further south. Bill Hoole, that mercurial figure from King's Cross, made his bow on the 'Non-Stop' in 1950, driving *Woodcock* on an eventful round trip on 26 and 27 June. On the Wednesday of that week he dropped ten minutes on the York–Grantham section due, according to his biography, to his fireman's inexperience in the firing methods required on the service, although a punctual arrival was still achieved. Mischance occurred on the Friday of that week when No. 60003 *Andrew K. McCosh* was found to have a broken middle piston-head at Hitchin – strangely enough, when taking water in preparation for re-routing via the Hertford loop.

A significant year for Britain was 1951, with the Festival on the Thames South Bank symbolizing the spirit of a nation attempting to claw its way out of the austere aftermath of war. It was also an important year for British Railways with the appearance of the first 'Standard' steam-engines, which were eventually to number one short of a round thousand by the time the last of them (No. 92220 *Evening Star*) was constructed in 1960. By that time there had been another change of policy, probably belatedly, to equip the network with diesel and electric traction.

Strangely enough, the 'Standard' steam locomotives do not enter our story at all, nor, even more strangely, will diesel locomotives, at least not on equal terms with steam engines. Instead, it was a minimal change in 1951 in locomotive deployment which had far-reaching consequences. This was the decision to allocate two crews to each 'top link' locomotive, as was already done north of the border, thus instilling a greater pride in the job.

Interestingly, it was a series of minor technical modifications, effectively nothing more than inexpensive tinkerings, which were to give the Gresley Pacifics an extended lease of life, especially the older A3s. These comprised the optical setting of valve gear, etc. and the later (almost too late) universal fitting of double-chimneys for the A3s and A4s.

A4s were now based only at King's Cross, Gateshead and Haymarket, those fitted with corridor tenders being allocated to the London and Edinburgh depots. King's Cross had no fewer than twenty streamliners (including the rebuilt W1) allocated that year, although not all of these were corridor tender fitted, while in contrast all of Haymarket's stud were capable of working a 'Non-Stop'.

Two weeks work on the 'Non-Stop' roster could involve no less than 145¾ hours work, giving a wage of £23 0s. 2d. per week, plus a lodging allowance of £2 12s. 9d. This was between three and four times the basic rate for a newly-passed driver at the time. Rates increased again in October 1951, sending a 'Non-Stop' driver's wage up to £27 17s. 3d.

The 'Capitals Limited' came down to a 440-minute timing for the London–Edinburgh distance in 1951, this being no mean schedule for a rake of 473 tons gross. The 'Flying Scotsman' took eighteen minutes longer for the journey, including stops at Grantham and Newcastle. Again, no punctuality figures for the 'Non-Stop' service appear to have been issued, and no particularly outstanding exploits apparently performed.

O.S. Nock made a footplate trip on the northbound 465-ton 'Limited' in 1951, when the usually reliable *Woodcock* gave her two firemen 'continual anxiety' because of poor steaming, and her drivers fought to overcome nearly twenty minutes of checks. It was a complete contrast to Nock's 1932 run on *Call Boy*; doubtless the coal supply was poorer and the permanent way more subject to delays from repairs and speed restrictions.

Official post-war figures for water consumption on the non-stop service make interesting reading. Starting with 5,000 gallons at the outset of the up journey, the

Her speed too high for the camera shutter to 'freeze', A4 No. 60024 *Kingfisher* sweeps the up 'Capitals Limited' through Cowton one summer around 1950. (Photomatic)

Pacifics' tender capacity was expected to be down to 2,350 gallons by Lucker, where an almost equal amount was picked up, 1,130 gallons by Wiske Moor, showing that this stretch was by far the most demanding in terms of water consumption, and down to only 750 gallons by Scrooby. These troughs near Doncaster obviously represented the most vital pick-up on the whole up run, but with only 1,400 gallons being 'scooped', emphasized the need for the next set of troughs, at Muskham, being only twenty-four miles farther on. Indeed, on this stretch the engine's water consumption was less than the amount picked up at Scrooby or the amount left unused by Muskham. From here on to King's Cross, expected to be reached with the tank quarter full, no water consumption problems were anticipated. There is no doubt that Wiske Moor–Scrooby was very much a 'water gap'; a maximum pick-up was obviously essential at both locations.

There was a further acceleration in 1952, when the summer service began on 30 June. This time the 'Capitals Limited' was only a few minutes outside the 'Flying Scotsman's' seven-hour timing of 1939. The new schedule of seven hours six minutes down and seven hours seven minutes up involved faster running on the Shaftesholme junction (Doncaster) to Berwick stretch than was the case pre-war. The train comprised eleven vehicles of around 400 tons tare, and punctuality was (unofficially) reported as being satisfactory. Up to the end of July, the 'Capitals Limited' was seen regularly passing Finsbury Park in the up direction a few minutes early, with Nos. 60017 *Silver Fox*, 60027 *Merlin* and No. 60033 *Seagull* prominent on the service.

By the end of the 'Non-Stop' season, 14 September, Nos. 60011/24/34 appear to have joined in the running of what was to be the last year of the 'Capitals Limited' before it was re-named. Verdicts differ as to whether the service was entirely trouble-free. The *Railway Magazine* announced that a clean sheet had been kept; another source declares that there was one failure due to faulty engine oil. Bill Hoole's biography attributes this failure to No. 60027 *Merlin* running hot almost as soon as Hoole had set foot on her footplate when taking over an up 'Non-Stop' at Tollerton, A2 Pacific No. 60521 *Watling Street* having to be substituted at York. Nevertheless, a sole locomotive failure was an acceptable statistic out of approximately 120 journeys. In defence of *Merlin*, it must be recorded that she operated twenty-eight consecutive 'Non-Stop's, followed, after a four day interval, by a further fourteen.

Evidence that work on the famous train was no sinecure can be found in P.W.B. Semmens' biography of Bill Hoole (see Bibliography). On one occasion in August 1952, Hoole's fireman had an arm injured by the water scoop handle while refuelling at Scrooby, but refused medical attention, either at the time, or while staying overnight in Edinburgh. His stoicism rebounded on all concerned the next day when, reporting for duty through the corridor tender, he proved unable to fire, an accompanying inspector having to set to work with a will. The fireman subsequently spent some time in hospital, and clearly should have sought help much earlier.

The best recorded performance on the train that year appears to come from the pen of Norman McKillop who credits Jimmy Swan on No. 60034 *Lord Faringdon* with regaining sixteen minutes of lost time north of York on the down service, including 90 mph down Cockburnspath bank. Obviously, this was a formidable achievement, given the tighter schedule already introduced on this stretch – not to mention the official 90 mph speed limit!

Indeed, it seems that BR administrators were convinced that there was room for

With eleven vehicles in tow and steam to spare, No. 60034 *Lord Faringdon* makes light work of the northbound train near Greenwood in September 1952. (J. Davenport)

Another class of ER locomotives not used on the non-stop runs were the massive A2 Pacifics which, with their 40,430 lb tractive effort, were, on paper at least, the most powerful of all the express passenger types. Seen in the twilight of its life, No. 60528 *Tudor Minstrel* pulls away from Aberdeen with the 09.10 a.m. to Edinburgh Waverley on 14 August 1965. (Courtney Haydon)

further accelerations, and, in a theoretical timing exercise for East Coast trains, a 377-minute schedule was postulated as being practicable for a London–Edinburgh non-stop service, provided the load was no more than 250 tons. This was not in fact to become reality, although it could be argued that the 'Talisman' services some four years later appear to have been built from this hypothesis, comprising early-morning and late-afternoon services in about six hours forty minutes with comparatively light loads and no more than three stops, by the end of the steam era.

The beginning of the end of non-stop running on Britain's railways occurred in 1953. With the death the previous year of the much-loved George VI, the nation was preparing for the coronation of a new monarch, his daughter Elizabeth. This resulted in the re-naming of the 'Capitals Limited' as 'The Elizabethan', a move much acclaimed at the time. In retrospect, it seems unfortunate to remove such an appropriate name from an express connecting non-stop the capital cities of England and Scotland. The new name could have been given to any train on the system, while it is no surprise to learn that within three years the Western Region adopted the geographically-explicit 'Capitals United' soubriquet for a London–Cardiff service.

The new 'Elizabethan' service started with another acceleration, this time breaking the seven hour barrier for the first time in the history of regular non-stop running. The new timing was $6\frac{3}{4}$ hours, requiring a 58 mph average with a standard rake of eleven coaches weighing 400 tons tare. The down train was allowed $189\frac{1}{2}$ minutes to York, including four minutes recovery time between Retford and Doncaster, the remaining $204\frac{3}{4}$ miles requiring $215\frac{1}{2}$ minutes. In the up direction, four minutes less was scheduled north of York, with four minutes inserted south of that point.

The permitted maximum on the East Coast was now 90 mph, giving crews a realistic chance of regaining any lost time if circumstances were favourable. The southern-most part of the run included no less than twenty-eight minutes for the seventeen miles from Hatfield to King's Cross, nine minutes more than the pre-war figure. Of course, there were still only two tracks for a good part of this approach to the capital, and delays could be expected by up trains at the height of summer. How these were sometimes dealt with will be recounted in due course.

The first down service of the 'Elizabethan' was powered by No. 60028 *Walter K. Whigham* on 29 June, reaching Edinburgh four minutes early. The corresponding up service, headed by No. 60009 *Union of South Africa*, was less fortunate. Driver Smith of King's Cross took over the southern half of the run punctually from Haymarket's Bill Stevenson but was unable to pick up water at Scrooby because of a water scoop failure, the resulting stop at Retford causing a $4\frac{1}{2}$-minute late arrival in London. Two days later Driver Smith, driving the same locomotive, scotched the memory of this unhappy inaugural run by bringing the train into King's Cross no less than $11\frac{1}{2}$ minutes early.

Observers noted Nos. 60017/28 operating the service as representatives of King's Cross in the earlier part of the summer season, while Haymarket rostered Nos. 60004/9/31. The record-breaking No. 60022 *Mallard* is recorded as having made only one trip in 1953, penetrating no farther north than Tweedmouth, where she had to be replaced. The date for this failure is not known, but Haymarket's No. 60004 *William Whitelaw* is known to have suffered a particularly embarrassing breakdown on 5 August, being removed from the down train only some thirty-eight miles out of King's Cross. A B1 4–6-0, No. 61203, was pressed into taking the train forward to Peterborough, where an unknown A4 took

On an overcast Edinburgh day, probably in 1953, King's Cross A4 No. 60028 *Walter K. Whigham* moves the up 'Elizabethan' out of Waverley station towards the Calton South tunnel past V2 No. 60949, waiting to take charge of a Waverley route express to Carlisle. (John Robertson)

over. Interestingly, in the absence of a corridor tender, the train made a special stop to change crews, proof that the 1932 memo, with its harsh ruling about both crews having to travel forward from the scene of the engine's replacement, was no longer valid.

Exactly a week later, on 12 August 1953, the northbound 'Elizabethan' was forced to stop at Hitchin for a coach dynamo belt to be adjusted, the express soon being seen passing Huntingdon some twenty-four minutes late. Undaunted, No. 60017 *Silver Fox* made a brilliant run on to Edinburgh, recovering all but three minutes, and averaging 63 mph for the 333 miles remaining. In contrast to these incident-ridden journeys, Bill Hoole, whose work on the 'Non-Stop' is better documented than any other driver pre- or post-war, made three uneventful round trips in August 1953. One of these journeys was with No. 60009 *Union of South Africa*, the other five with its Haymarket stable-mate No. 60011 *Empire of India*. An up journey with the latter culminated in a most unusual ending.

Around this time, the northern approach to King's Cross was coming under critical attention, with a dire need for quadrupled lines for as much as possible of the East Coast line south of Hatfield. Proof that suburban congestion was affecting express traffic both in theory and practice was not hard to find. The final seventeen miles southwards from Hatfield was effectively timetabled with some ten minutes recovery time to allow for delay – and with good reason. One up Saturday service of the 'Capitals Limited' in 1951 took no less than seventy-five minutes to travel the last $8\frac{1}{4}$ miles from Oakleigh Park, arriving almost empty at King's Cross as most passengers had transferred to the Underground at Finsbury Park! Two years later, with the congestion still un-relieved, the

One of King's Cross' best – A4 No. 60032 *Gannet* speeds through Croft Spa on the beginning of the Darlington–York 'racing stretch' with the up 'Elizabethan' in July 1954. (Photomatic)

up 'Elizabethan' was re-routed onto the slow line at Cemetery box on 22 August, so that Driver Hoole, in charge of *Empire of India*, could overtake two Yorkshire expresses awaiting entry to the terminus. Thus the 'crack' express made a punctual arrival, albeit at the expense of what the railway management evidently regarded as 'provincial' traffic. One wonders what Yorkshire passengers made of that.

As the first summer of the 'Elizabethan' turned to autumn, the 'Non-Stop's' stock took on the guise of the 'Flying Scotsman', enlarged as required. Although the summer composition of the train was described as being entirely air-conditioned, this was not strictly true, certainly not in 1954. Three of the eleven vehicles, the First class restaurant-kitchen car, luggage brake and Aberdeen brake-composite, did not have such a refinement, although the first two had side panelling below the solebars to match the air-conditioned stock. On Saturdays the buffet lounge, described by one writer as 'a most palatial vehicle, a triumph of the British coachbuilder's craft', and one brake, were replaced with three extra passenger vehicles to increase capacity. The two buffet cars ran between London and Edinburgh on other services each weekend, being returned to the 'Elizabethan' for the following Monday.

'A truly lamentable exhibition.' That was C.J. Allen's experience of one of his two 'Elizabethan' journeys in 1954, a year when he averred that the train 'cannot be said to have covered itself with its wonted glory'. Another traveller, R.S. Watson, made one unpunctual up trip in August 1954 when No. 60031 *Golden Plover* had to stop for water at Darlington, something that should have been prevented as the problem, a leaking tender tank, was obvious even to non-railwaymen on the departure platform at Waverley, when the substitute engine should surely have been called for. On the other hand, A.S. Haddon made five round trips on the 1954 services, every one of them terminating ahead of scheduled time. Both of Allen's journeys will be examined in due course, but no introduction to 1954 can possibly overlook a number of milestones.

First among these was the acceleration to the fastest-ever timing for an Anglo–Scottish non-stop service – 6½ hours. For the first time this distance had to be averaged at more than a mile-a-minute. This was a magnificent testimony to the excellence of the Gresley A4s, four of which were now approaching their twentieth year, an age when their 'Deltic' successors would be considered obsolete. Not only that, but one such Pacific would run no fewer than *sixty-one* journeys on this accelerated schedule.

Even before the new timing was introduced on 28 June, the 1954 'season' had started with a new record bid. In order to celebrate the holding of the International Railway Congress in Britain, the delegates were taken from London to Edinburgh in two special expresses on Saturday 22 May, each scheduled to make the journey non-stop. Shades of the LNWR Euston–Carlisle run of 1903! The trains, powered respectively by No. 60022 *Mallard* and No. 60034 *Lord Faringdon*, were scheduled to complete the journey in 6¾ hours, at the 'Elizabethan's' 1953 timing, but leaving King's Cross within ten minutes of each other, at 7.55 a.m. and 8.05 a.m. The 'Coronation' observation cars brought up the rear of each special.

It would be pleasant to record that this extraordinary double non-stop run was an unqualified success, but it was not to be. *Mallard* reached Waverley four minutes early, but the second special fell foul of the Wiske Moor pumping mechanism which had so worried Gresley more than a quarter of a century before. Failing to scoop up enough water at the troughs, *Lord Faringdon* was forced to take refreshment at Darlington, and her (his?) arrival status at Edinburgh was not recorded. As ten minutes should have been sufficient leeway between the trains to ensure the refilling of the troughs – it obviously was for five out of the six – it is possible that the second train was gaining on the first and that headway between them was reduced, perhaps even halved. Nevertheless, it was an interesting introduction to an eventful summer – whatever 'CJA' was to say.

BR's confidence in the A4's ability to deliver their trains on time was fully justified as the opening accelerated services proved. No. 60030 *Golden Fleece* reached Edinburgh three minutes early on 28 June, while its northern counterpart *Union of South Africa* was into King's Cross with five minutes to spare. The new 60 mph service gave a 5.55 p.m. arrival in Dundee, while Aberdeen was reached by a quarter to eight. The Saturday service was now timed for seven hours three minutes (down) and seven hours seven minutes (up), including a stop at Newcastle. This was very much a concession to reality, the Saturday services being so subject to delays from excursion and other summer-only traffic as to be almost unworkable non-stop.

By the end of July, only Nos. 60030/32 had been rostered from the southern end, while No.60009 was beginning her marathon contribution of sixty-one journeys from the north. This was to include an unbroken spell from 5 August to 11 September. The *Union* even had the consideration to complete an up journey on 19 July before revealing that she had developed a hot box! This same engine, now thankfully preserved, had the honour of

With a wave from her Scottish fireman, A4 No. 60028 *Walter K. Whigham* accelerates through Darlington onto the forty-four-mile 'racing stretch' towards York on the up 'Elizabethan' around 1954. Note how much coal is visible on the top of the tender nearly half-way through the journey. (Photomatic)

being timed by Cecil J. Allen on one of his two 'Elizabethan' journeys in 1954, and in saying that she reached her destination more than 2½ hours late, it must be added that this was no fault of the locomotive.

With a 420-ton gross load, the down journey saw time being dropped all the way, despite the forty-four miles between York and Darlington being covered in thirty-eight minutes and nineteen seconds. Durham was passed nine minutes late, and then, to Allen's surprise and dismay, the 'Elizabethan' was diverted across the Tyne by the High Level Bridge before taking the Carlisle line. A freight derailment in Northumberland had ensured that Mr Allen and his fellow-passengers were in for a refresher course in convoluted diversions, Falahill included.

Running without taking water between Wiske Moor and Carlisle, the A4 took fifteen minutes to re-fill her tender in the Citadel station, before heading for the Waverley Route. Taking 162 minutes for the ninety-eight miles thence to Edinburgh compares somewhat badly with the Holmes 4–4–0 which once raced over this notorious route in only 126 minutes during the Race of 1901, albeit with only 150 tons. Surprisingly, the crew on this 1954 journey deemed it necessary to stop for banking assistance for the Whitrope climb, another ten miles or so at around 1 in 75, but a climb quite within the power of the engine provided she was not starting from cold. Indeed, only one coach-length away from the J36 0–6–0 'banker', Allen professed himself unable to hear its exhaust, underlining many a Waverley Route engineman's suspicion that the Whitrope and Falahill banking units only attached themselves for the ride!

Through no fault of her own, *Union of South Africa* had distinctly failed to impress this doyen of railway journalists, who was presumably too busy timing the train to appreciate the border scenery that BR were laying on without addition to the fare. The up 'Elizabethan' was similarly diverted that day, taking water at St. Boswells and Carlisle, reaching King's Cross 159 minutes late. We know that on at least one occasion when the southbound 'Non-Stop' was diverted through Carlisle, the crews attempted to run right through from there to London with only the briefest of stops, possibly even a mere slowing to walking pace, to drop the pilotman at Newcastle (Haymarket crews would not normally work over the Newcastle–Carlisle route). If successful, and details are unfortunately vague, this would represent a most creditable 328-mile distance accomplished non-stop, again, as in 1948, at the instigation of the footplatemen themselves.

As if to rub salt in the wounds, the up 'Elizabethan' on which Allen returned to London two days later also gave an unpunctual arrival, and gave rise to the 'lamentable' comment. No. 60008 *Dwight D. Eisenhower* had 430 tons gross behind her and covered the North Eastern 'racing ground' between Darlington and York pass-to-pass in thirty-seven minutes and twenty-one seconds, but was some twenty minutes late by Doncaster. Out-of-course checks appeared to stifle any effort by the engine crew to regain time and Allen claims he found himself apologizing for the delays to American fellow passengers who had chosen to travel by the 'Elizabethan' under the impression that it was a 'crack' express.

Allen, writing in *Trains Illustrated*, blamed the drivers concerned for not recovering quickly enough from delays, citing as an inspiration Ted Hailstone's effort that year in running from London to Rossington, 151 miles in 138 minutes, to recover seven minutes on this most difficult schedule. This included spurring his engine, No. 60032 *Gannet*, to cover the 12.2 miles from Hitchin to Sandy in eight minutes and four seconds – an average of 90.8 mph. With Swan taking over in Yorkshire, the much-delayed 'Elizabethan' reached Waverley two minutes early, after a final 'ninety' down Cockburnspath. Perhaps Allen's was an unfair comment; no two trips with a steam engine were ever the same from one day to the next, or even one hour to the next, particularly when handled by two different crews during the length of a single long-distance journey.

But the year did include a 'brilliant performance'. Again it was Bill Hoole who kept the standard flying with a 164-minute nett run from York to King's Cross, on the 19 July up 'Elizabethan'. What made this all the more creditable was the fact that his engine, No. 60024 *Kingfisher*, was a last minute replacement for the rostered locomotive and suffered injector trouble just north of York. (Strange how failures seemed to come to light when the replacement crew took over – as with *Merlin* in 1952 – possibly because the new footplatemen immediately detected a vibration, a smell or some other tell-tale symptom that had escaped the attention of crewmen tired at the end of their shift.)

On this occasion Driver Smith of Haymarket had played his part very creditably, taking over a reserve engine at short notice and handing over to his London counterpart only $1\frac{3}{4}$ minutes late after negotiating three major permanent way slowings. Hoole made a temporary stop, costing nearly five minutes, in order to tackle the injector problem beneath footplate level, and York was passed some eight minutes late. This was the kind of challenge this 'engineman extraordinary' relished, and the replacement engine almost took wing down Stoke Bank, reaching 100 mph on one of the few recorded occasions on this service. The twenty-nine miles between Grantham and Peterborough was recorded by G.W. Goslin as having taken only $21\frac{3}{4}$ minutes, with 94 mph being averaged for more than fifteen miles. London was reached punctually at 4.15 p.m., itself something of a logistical achievement given that there were arrivals scheduled ahead of the 'Elizabethan' at 4.03 p.m. from Ripon, 4.07 p.m. from Cambridge and 4.13 p.m. from Peterborough. So if 1954 was a poor year, it was at least brightened by a 100 mph dash of halcyon blue, figuratively speaking.

The following year, 1955, was a better one for the 'Non-Stop'; indeed, one of the best. Not a single engine failure was recorded in the contemporary technical press. Up to the end of July punctuality was described as 'exemplary'.

It was a summer when No. 60033 *Seagull* made fifty trips between the capitals, her sister (if that is not an inappropriate gender), *Lord Faringdon* contributing twenty-four individual journeys, the most prolific Haymarket A4 being No. 60031 *Golden Plover* with eighteen. The usual twosome from the northern end, *Union of South Africa* and *Merlin*, did not figure so prominently as usual, although they headed both down and up trains respectively on 16 July, when No. 60034 *Lord Faringdon* of King's Cross was stopped at Haymarket for attention. Conversely, London engines, No. 60013 *Dominion of New Zealand* and *Seagull* headed both services exactly one week later, the former deputizing for a 'stopped' Scottish Pacific.

The above statistics included Sunday journeys, the 'Elizabethan' engines working through between the capitals at weekends with the 9.34 a.m. down and 9.45 a.m up on Saturdays, and 10.00 a.m. down and 10.50 a.m. up on Sundays. On these occasions the crew-changing was carried out through the corridor tender, despite a stop being made at Newcastle. On weekdays the King's Cross standby A4 would, if not required on the 'Non-Stop', work the 12.18 p.m. to Grantham, returning with the up 'White Rose'.

Before the summer started, water scoops were modified to dip an extra $\frac{3}{4}$ in to improve water collection, No. 60028 making two unusual spring visits to Edinburgh on 22 March and 24 April 1955 to test the new arrangements. Meanwhile, the 'Flying Scotsman', which had started the fashion for long-distance record-breaking, was back to a non-stop schedule between King's Cross and Newcastle. Everything was set for a good year on the ECML.

The first notable run occurred on 11 July on the down 'Elizabethan'. No. 60034 *Lord Faringdon* dropped some seventeen minutes on schedule by York with the mystified recorder noting that the engine was allowed to blow off when on the easier stretches. Despite the efforts of Jimmy Swan and Fireman Booth, who took over north of York, another three minutes were lost before Newcastle, but north of the Tyne things were different. A brilliant run through Northumberland brought the 425-ton train to Berwick in four seconds over the even hour and there was an exceptionally high 80 mph average over the thirty miles further north from Cockburnspath to Inveresk.

Unfortunately, Edinburgh Control had not expected a potential twenty-minute recovery on a '60 mph-plus' timing over only 124.5 miles, and the express was delayed at Joppa. Nevertheless, the 113 minutes 2 seconds for the Newcastle–Edinburgh distance pass-to-stop was magnificent, and was achieved, Swan later informed author Norman McKillop, by using 15 per cent reverser most of the way and 'hardly any fuel'. If this last comment seems a predictable exaggeration from a biased Gresley engine-driver, it certainly accords with the report that, on one unspecified date during the 'Elizabethan' years, Driver Edwards on *Seagull* brought the up train into King's Cross five minutes early with three tons of coal still on the tender.

But Haymarket men were not the only crews setting the lineside heather on fire, figuratively speaking. On 21 July Driver Hailstone of King's Cross ran No. 60013 *Dominion of New Zealand* on the down train in eighteen minutes and thirty-six seconds between Hitchin and Huntingdon, an average of 87.1 mph, including 96 mph at Arlesey. York was reached in only 175 minutes, whereupon Hailstone's successor, Driver Gemmell of Haymarket, made a point of averaging 90 mph over the 13.9 miles between Pilmoor and Northallerton, putting the 425-ton 'Elizabethan' ten minutes ahead of time.

But Ted Hailstone was not to be outdone and on 29 August took the up train through Grantham at 76 mph and over Stoke Summit with a loss of only 10 mph. With the twenty miles from Newark up to Summit being run in an incredible fifteen minutes and forty-one seconds, including the uphill stretch, the train was $5\frac{1}{2}$ minutes early by Peterborough. King's Cross was reached some seven minutes to the good, in a nett time of little more than six hours. Jimmy Swan was the other driver responsible for this fine effort, and the much underrated *Seagull* the engine.

The following day this fine locomotive took wing again, this time with Bill Hoole at the controls. Stoke was breasted in the northbound direction at 70 mph, Grantham, 105 miles in ninety-seven minutes and forty-one seconds, $5\frac{3}{4}$ minutes early. An earlier collision between an up train and a tractor at Ranskill put the 'Elizabethan' $11\frac{1}{4}$ minutes down by Doncaster, but Hoole had recovered $2\frac{1}{2}$ minutes by York, where Driver Swan completed the equation, taking *Seagull* through Newcastle less than three minutes late, and a $1\frac{1}{4}$-minute early arrival recorded at Waverley. The recorder, Mr Ronald Nelson, estimated a nett time of only five minutes over six hours.

In admiring these high-speed exploits, it seems puzzling in retrospect that the load was not reduced by two coaches to around 330 tons tare and a six-hour schedule introduced. It would have involved only 18 tons more than the pre-war 'Coronation', to be hauled without time being lost for stops. It could undoubtedly have been done, and with such men as Hoole, Hailstone and Swan to operate it, failure to accelerate the 'Elizabethan' can only be seen, and not just in retrospect, as a lost opportunity.

The modern rail enthusiast has to bear in mind that these near six-hour nett times were being achieved with 425 tons of trailing load, roughly the equivalent of eight empty IC125 carriages. Of course, in contrast to the 5,000 bhp which the present-day twin diesels can bring to bear on their trains, an A4 Pacific, fired by one man over a four-hour shift, could hardly hope to muster more than a shade above 40 per cent of this power output over any kind of sustained period. Obviously, A4s were recorded as producing higher power outputs over a short distance, but only at the expense of 'mortgaging' the boiler.

And still *Seagull*'s achievements accumulated. On 26 July she passed Hatfield, 375 miles from Edinburgh, in $366\frac{1}{4}$ minutes on an up 'Non-stop', including a $35\frac{3}{4}$-minute timing on the North Eastern 'racing stretch'. One rail enthusiast, newly returned from a long exile abroad, was captivated by the sight of this engine arriving (early) at King's Cross one day in 1955 on the 'Elizabethan', describing *Seagull* as being 'much more than impeccably clean. She had what could only be described as a pre-1914 gleam about her . . . a sight to gladden an exile's heart.'

Nor did her appearance mislead. The *Railway Magazine* records, unfortunately without giving a date, an occasion, probably in August 1955, when this engine, arrived non-stop that day from Edinburgh, was turned out by King's Cross to head a 10.20 p.m.

One of the finest performers on the 'Non-Stop' duty was A4 No. 60033 *Seagull*, seen accelerating down Cockburnspath bank through the Berwickshire hills with the Edinburgh-bound 'Elizabethan' in 1954. After working successfully on the former GWR lines in the 1948 Exchange trials, a Western Region inspector reportedly said of *Seagull*, 'We have nothing to touch this engine.' Praise indeed! (John Robertson)

relief as far as Grantham, returning to London at around five in the morning. She was promptly turned around again on the down 'Elizabethan'! This would give a mileage since the previous morning only four miles short of a thousand, in no more than thirty-one hours.

Nineteen fifty-five closed with a new high-powered diesel locomotive beginning trials on BR. Constructed by English Electric as a private initiative, the 3,300 bhp 'Deltic' was destined to provide the Gresley A4s with a more powerful successor, capable of intensive utilization and high mileage. Ironically, as will be seen, the production 'Deltics' were not to figure in the non-stop story; indeed their introduction may have directly caused its cessation.

The following year, 1956, was the last when the 'Elizabethan' – or any other train – was scheduled to average more than 60 mph between the English and Scottish capitals for some six years. Just as the blue and white 3,300 hp diesel was a portent of things to come, so was the beginning of the rebuilding of Potters Bar station and adjacent tunnels. While ultimately offering a minimum of four tracks in and out of King's Cross from the northern approaches, the short-term price to be paid would be deceleration from 1957, certainly in the case of the 'Elizabethan'. Interestingly, in contrast to 1939, when the

Prototype of the 'Deltic' diesels which would later oust the A4s from their role at the head of the 'Elizabethan', which immediately lost its 'Non-Stop' character, owing to the lack of communicating doors in the nose of the production models. The diesel is seen at Peterborough North in February 1959 sporting its distinctive blue, silver and yellow livery. Despite being ignored by the enthusiasts at the time of their introduction the 'Deltics' would later command a considerable following with the prototype now preserved at the Science Museum in South Kensington. (Philip Kelley)

heavy non-stop 'Flying Scotsman' was required to maintain a mile-a-minute schedule between King's Cross and Grantham (105 miles), the 1956 'Elizabethan' was granted three minutes over two hours over the same stretch, an indication of how civil engineering works close to the capital were slowing journeys, while, in contrast, some of the northern stretches were losing their easy-going character.

Unlike the previous year, the first month of non-stop running in 1956 was not auspicious. While No. 60010 *Dominion of Canada* made an uneventful northbound trip, No. 60012 *Commonwealth of Australia* of Haymarket had a delayed first up journey, apparently then being taken off the roster by King's Cross, which found the engine able enough to head the 'White Rose' on successive days. Nevertheless the season (from 25 June to 16 September) was to be completed with only one mechanical failure *en route*; No. 60030 *Golden Fleece* being removed from the down train at Newcastle on 4 July, her poor steaming caused by inferior coal, although as standby engine she may have taken over the working in less than a peak of readiness. Most prolific unit on the 'Elizabethan' that year was No. 60011 *Empire of India* with fifty-seven runs, despite not being regarded as the best of the A4s, and *Seagull*, which certainly deserved to be, having operated fifty-six.

The latter engine produced one of the few 'tons'(100 mph) of the 'Non-Stop's' history when she took the usual eleven coach, 425-ton gross load southwards over Stoke at

Haymarket depot reputedly hand-coaled A4 Pacifics for the 'Non-Stop' duty, but No. 60011 *Empire of India* seems to have a lot of slack on top of her bunker as she leaves the depot for Waverley and the 393-mile run to London (King's Cross) in 1957. In 1956 this engine is believed to have achieved fifty-seven consecutive journeys on the 'Elizabethan' and its weekend equivalents. (D.A. Anderson)

around 70 mph before notching 100 mph at Essendine and averaging 93.2 mph over the 15.2 miles between Corby and Helpston. She was five minutes early by Hitchin and this lengthened to 7½ minutes by the terminus, despite a delayed approach. The nett time recorded was, again, only five minutes over six hours, the crew Driver Hailstone and Fireman Law. Interestingly, the train had not been running late when this feat of speed occurred, the recorder describing it as nothing less than *joie de vivre*.

Even the routine journeys on this 60 mph schedule over a record distance were exceptional, if that does not sound illogical. S.C. Crowther-Smith made a down journey around this time which began with No. 60024 *Kingfisher* coming to a standstill for an unspecified reason in Copenhagen tunnel, only yards from her starting-point. Despite this, Peterborough was passed in seventy-five minutes and Doncaster in 152. The York–Darlington 'racing stretch' was taken sedately in forty-two minutes, still above the 60 mph average, and Newcastle passed eight minutes short of 4½ hours. Mr Crowther-Smith noticed unusually high speeds north of Grantshouse, with gradients in the train's favour, but Waverley was not quite ready for the train, holding it at Piershill, at the foot of 1¼ miles at 1 in 78. Nevertheless, the Scottish capital was reached 1½ minutes early. The traveller's reaction? 'A train of which Britain can be very proud.'

Down non-stop expresses from King's Cross began their 393-mile journeys with a challenging climb through the Gas Works and Copenhagen tunnels at 1 in 107, with a subsequent easing to 1 in 200 for the remaining ten miles or so to Potter's Bar. Here, A4 No. 60030 *Golden Fleece* makes the climb with an unidentified train, passing King's Cross depot to the right of the picture. (Philip Kelley)

In contrast to King's Cross, southbound trains from Waverley 'launched' themselves down 1¼ miles of 1 in 78 to the site of St Margaret's depot, which A4 No. 60032 *Gannet* is here seen passing, watched by two railwaymen. The engine is hauling a stopping express, an unusual task for a King's Cross engine in Scotland before the 'Deltic' era caused re-allocations. (Courtney Haydon)

Another unexceptional trip which still made fascinating reading in the railway press was a footplate journey made by W.J. Alcock on a southbound 'Elizabethan' on 16 August that year. Accompanied by an inspector, the lucky traveller began his footplate visit at Northallerton shortly before the crews changed over at Tollerton in the course of a thirty-six minutes and twenty-three seconds passage of the 'racing stretch'. Mr Alcock found the corridor tender 'exciting' to negotiate, emerging from near-darkness on to the footplate of No. 60011 *Empire of India* 'rocking and swaying southwards at 78 mph'. In fact the locomotive's riding was a source of comment, this particular A4 showing a tendency to 'hunt' at more than 80 mph, a problem Alcock was assured was not typical of the class.

The Haymarket fireman handed over a fine fire to his southern counterpart, who emerged from the train a few minutes before his driver. The engine was driven throughout on full regulator and 15 per cent cut-off whenever possible, but with Stoke Bank being topped at 55 mph, and 88 mph reached down the other side, *Empire of India* had to be eased nearing the capital, where a 6½-minute early arrival was recorded. The privileged footplate traveller reckoned that the timetable allowed an effective twenty-minute margin in good conditions, this with the 400-plus ton gross load. The crewmen on this occasion were drivers Stevenson and Tappin, and firemen Wallace-Fyfe and Bright. The accompanying official was Inspector Goodhand, who believed that the engine could have gone on, the railway system and water supplies permitting, to reach Bournemouth!

Ironically, with the 'Elizabethan' crying out for a lightening of its load to make a six-hour London–Edinburgh timing feasible, the Eastern, North Eastern and Scottish managements decided to introduce a new lightweight (eight-coach) service between the cities, entitled 'The Talisman'. This left each city at 4.00 p.m., stopping only at Newcastle, and was timed for six hours forty minutes. Over the next few years, the formula would be altered, counterbalancing morning services being introduced to give the first-ever daily return working between the capitals for the rolling stock, and an increase in the coaching rake due to popularity. This was particularly true in the case of the up morning and down evening services, the former at one time of the train's career beginning its journey at Perth and temporarily bearing the name 'The Fair Maid'.

But what a lost opportunity! The first 'Talisman' rake included two saloons from the 'Coronation' but with overall greater passenger capacity. Surely an equally short 'Elizabethan' was an obvious need, trimmed to a six hour schedule?

Nineteen fifty-six should not be left without a mention of the floods of 28 August. Yet again the Scottish Borders were inundated by a cloudburst which closed the ECML at Grantshouse. Powered by *Empire of India*, the 'Elizabethan' headed south over the Waverley Route, regaining her usual itinerary after passing through Carlisle and Hexham. According to one report, No. 60011 was removed at Newcastle for an unspecified reason, No. 60016 *Silver King* bringing the train into London. However, following trains, including the 'Flying Scotsman', were not so lucky. Two of them were turned round before travelling more than half the Waverley line, being forced to return to Edinburgh because of suspected subsidence, and then had to reverse on to former Caledonian metals to take the West Coast main line. The unfortunate up 'Scotsman' was photographed passing Crawford, only some forty-five miles out from Edinburgh, *five hours* after leaving! It was all so reminiscent of 1948.

The day's down 'Elizabethan' was headed over Beattock by *Seagull*, which was able to work southwards the next day over the re-opened Waverley Route, while on the 30th the train was seen back on the ECML, piloted up Cockburnspath by a D34 'Glen' 4-4-0. Once again the train engine was *Empire of India*, observed passing Newcastle half-an-hour late. She was reported to have regained seventeen minutes from there to London, Driver Smith bringing her up to the capital from York in 169 minutes. The next day his King's Cross colleague, Driver Guymer, knocked two minutes off this timing at the regulator of the ever-impressive *Seagull*.

The non-stop season of 1956 closed with a September journey of the up 'Elizabethan' arriving one minute late at King's Cross despite being hampered by no fewer than nine delays. No. 60027 *Merlin* had spread her wings down Stoke Bank, running her 430-ton train at an average of 90.5 mph between Little Bytham and Tallington, and her crews, drivers Nairn and Hailstone and firemen McKay and Bottomley, had achieved a 372 minute nett time.

It is not just with the addition of hindsight that the 1957 re-timetabling of the 'Elizabethan' – to 395 minutes – seems puzzling. One contemporary railway journalist pointed out that only two minutes cut from the new schedule would have given BR the opportunity of continuing to advertise the train as a 'mile-a-minute' express. There was no longer a single train in or out of King's Cross which could make such a claim. In particular, the 'Elizabethan', with its new timing of six hours thirty-five minutes failed by only a few minutes to provide a connection at Waverley for the 4.00 p.m. to Perth and Inverness, thus missing the chance of an excellent daytime service from London to the Highland capital. It was an uninspired episode of apparently negative timing.

A3s gave way to A4s on the East Coast 'Non-Stop', rendering appropriate this pairing of light engines leaving Haymarket for Waverley in 1958. The 'Elizabethan's engine, A4 No. 60011 *Empire of India*, is equipped with a double-chimney, an improvement yet to be fitted to the leading engine, A3 No. 60083 *Sir Hugo*, based at Heaton depot at this time. (D.A. Anderson)

Part of the problem seems to have sprung from the need to incorporate extra time into train schedules to allow for delays caused by civil engineering operations. The Eastern Region appears to have been in considerable confusion as to how much recovery time to allow East Coast trains, erring on the side of caution, just as the LMR were soon to do with diesel-hauled expresses on the West Coast during the process of electrification, when London residents intending to greet friends would often find that the train they were to meet at Euston had already arrived an hour earlier. Something similar is happening on the East Coast main line during its electrification metamorphosis at the time of writing. So perhaps inexperience in fixing recovery time margins can be employed as an excuse for the deceleration on the East Coast in 1956–7. On Guy Fawkes Day in 1956, for example, Driver Hoole made up nearly half an hour on the new 'Talisman' service northwards on No. 60026 *Miles Beevor*.

There was, however, no excuse whatever for BR slowness in modifying the streamlined A4 Pacifics with double-chimneys. Only four of the class had been so equipped from their construction, yet the exploits of *Seagull* alone, if not *Mallard*, should have provided ample evidence of an improved performance for minimal cost. It was only by the end of 1958 that the whole class had been converted, the last two being Nos. 60009/32, ironically two of the most frequent performers on the 'Non-Stop'.

As if to emphasize the benefits of the much-delayed improvement, the newly-equipped

Believed to be the record holder for the number of 'Non-Stops' (and weekend balancing rosters) run in a single season – more than seventy – A4 No. 60012 *Commonwealth of Australia* is seen here powering a mid-1950s Glasgow express westwards out of Edinburgh. (D.A. Anderson)

The magnificent lines of the A4 are captured to advantage with this broadside view of No. 60010 *Dominion of Canada* near Oakleigh Park in 1960. This engine was formally named *Woodcock*, a name which was later transferred to sister locomotive No. 60029. (Courtney Haydon)

No. 60017 *Silver Fox* climbed Stoke Bank at an average of 83 mph *uphill* for 15.3 miles, reaching Grantham in ninety-eight minutes, on the 'Morning Talisman' of 25 June 1957. The older A3s were also granted a new lease of life with the double-chimney arrangements, soon finding themselves restored to the 'Flying Scotsman', the only resulting problem being drifting smoke, later rectified by the fitting of German-design 'elephant's ears' smoke deflectors.

The 1957 non-stop season began on 17 June but does not appear to have produced any outstanding runs, nor were punctuality statistics released. Indeed, it was the West Coast which was producing the star performances. Not only did the new lightweight 'Caledonian' express produce an *actual* 363-minute journey between Glasgow (Central) and Euston on 5 September 1957, but the winter time 299-mile timetabling between London and Carlisle was the new non-stop record run for Britain during the winter months.

The year also saw the retirement of Ted Hailstone, a driver who seemed to be able to draw a maximum performance from a steam engine without thrashing it or exhausting the fireman – an art soon to be lost as new motive power made its value a forgotten currency.

With the 'Elizabethan' dropping below the 60 mph standard, rail enthusiasts' attention seemed to centre more on the train's locomotive failures, rather than its timekeeping successes. The double record-breaker *Mallard* made a down trip in early July 1957 that was completed $1\frac{1}{2}$ minutes early despite some twenty-four minutes of delays. However, on

Appropriately named after the designer, No. 60007 *Sir Nigel Gresley* is here seen on shed at Doncaster. This is one of several members of the A4 class now preserved, which can be seen operating special trains on BR from time to time. Regretfully, none of these are on the route of the former 'Non-Stop'. (Courtney Haydon)

the 5th of the month, after touching 97 mph at Essendine, she ran hot and had to come off the up service at Peterborough. Her replacement was V2 2-6-2 No. 60897 which covered the 73.8 miles to passing Finsbury Park in 72½ minutes, despite two permanent way slowings. Arrival at the terminus was nineteen minutes late, although delays had amounted to nearly twice as much.

The outstanding contribution to the 'Non-Stop' that year appears to have come from Haymarket's No. 60012 *Commonwealth of Australia*. From the first day of the service, 17 June, she seems to have worked continuously until 21 August, when shedmate No. 60027 *Merlin* deputized for her, and the former engine was recorded back working on the train in the second week of September. One report debits 'No. 12' with having failed on the down train near Gateshead on 20 August, being replaced by A2 No. 60538 *Velocity* which was seen passing Newcastle Central thirty-five minutes late. Certainly *Merlin* was on the up train next day, passing through Central five minutes early. It would be interesting to have confirmation of *Commonwealth of Australia*'s unbroken record of non-stop running, which the author calculates as sixty-five successive rosterings (including through weekend workings) up to 21 August.

Merlin deputized again on 28 August, this time for the London Pacific No. 60015 *Quicksilver*, the latter being stopped at Haymarket for a couple of days. A few days later King's Cross took Haymarket's *Union of South Africa* off the roster, its substitute

curiously enough being reported as No. 60016 *Silver King*; as this A4 lost its corridor tender in 1948, one of her London-based 'silver' sisters was a more probable replacement.

The 1958 non-stop season began on 9 June, when No. 60030 *Golden Fleece* and No. 60031 *Golden Plover*, headed the down and up 'Elizabethan's respectively. With numerous signal delays being encountered by *Golden Fleece*, the down train was into Waverley nineteen minutes late, the connecting Aberdeen service having to leave in a reserve 'path' thirty-five minutes late, with a further five minutes being lost to Dundee. Up to mid-August, Nos. 60013/21/30/33 appeared from the southern end, the second of these (*Wild Swan*) having been allocated the corridor tender the previous year from No. 60008 *Dwight D. Eisenhower*, while Haymarket rostered Nos. 60012/27/31. The timing was the same, but the times were not.

King's Cross top link now comprised no fewer than forty crews, none of them rostered a particular locomotive. Ted Hailstone's old mount, *Silver Link*, was reckoned to have run 30,000 fewer miles in the year since her famous driver's retirement than in his last twelve months at the regulator, principally as a result of this arguably false economy in the adoption of the common user system.

Of course, all this may have had something to do with the introduction of the English Electric Type 4s (later Class 40s), which, from the start of the summer, began heading some of the East Coast's most important trains, including the 'Flying Scotsman'. Not that these units were paradigms of intensive utilization to begin with. Just as the German railway managers had discovered the difficulties of integrating the 'Flying Hamburger' diesel trains into a steam-orientated railway system in the 1930s, so did their British East Coast counterparts encounter problems. By November 1958 not one of the five Class 40s allocated to the former Great Northern lines was working to its planned diagram. But their steam shedmates were little better; the *Railway Observer* reported that no fewer than forty main-line locomotives were unavailable at the height of the August holiday season on the Great Northern section alone.

Looking back, it is difficult for the non-professional railway historian to interpret the real nature of those final 1950s years on the ECML. For every outstanding run behind steam power, there was a balancing tale of breakdown. On 10 July 1958 *Golden Fleece* lost her scoop, possibly from 'dipping' at too fast a speed, being replaced *en route* on the up 'Elizabethan' by York's A2/2 No. 60503 *Lord President*, itself originally one of Gresley's P2s which paved the way for the A4s. Later up 'Elizabethan's reached King's Cross from Peterborough behind V2s Nos. 60817 and 60852 within the passage of six days, but in none of these cases was the lateness of the arrival recorded.

On the other hand, a down journey around this time saw No. 60013 *Dominion of New Zealand* take the 425 gross tonnage of the 'Elizabethan' northwards with an average of 87 mph between Hitchin and Huntingdon (in eighteen minutes and sixteen seconds!) and achieve the round 'ton' at Arlesey.

The single most important event in 1958 in the history of the ECML was the order placed in May for twenty-one 'Deltic' diesels, although in the three years before they would begin appearing on the line, and the four before they began a properly accelerated service, steam still had some running to do.

The 1959 non-stop season began on 15 June, with No. 60015 *Quicksilver* heading the down 'Elizabethan' and No. 60011 *Empire of India* the up. In fact, by the end of the

summer Nos. 60027/8 were to be the most regular performers (on the same 395-minute timing), with the former of these two, *Merlin*, notching up sixty-two journeys between the capitals, and the other, *Walter K. Whigham*, achieving fifty-three. Other A4s showing their mettle were Nos. 60033/4 from King's Cross (as well as No. 60007 *Sir Nigel Gresley* which made two trips), and No. 60031 *Golden Plover* from Haymarket, in addition to the two noted on the first day.

Two failures 'on the road' were recorded, both involving London-based engines developing injector trouble and having to be taken off the up service at Peterborough. On these occasions, on 22 June and 17 August respectively, V2s Nos. 60914 and 60928 deputised. No Haymarket engines failed *en route*, prompting one technical journalist to comment, 'From this record it is clear that Haymarket still maintains its locos in fine mechanical condition.' Indeed, in the four summers 1958–61, not one Haymarket engine failed on the actual 'Non-Stop', suggesting either that fitters were easier to recruit in Edinburgh, or that the Scottish depot's policy of allocating as few A4s as possible to the service – and giving them priority in the maintenance 'pecking order' – was paying dividends.

Mention has been made of No. 60007 *Sir Nigel Gresley*, an engine which is still (for this fine A4 is preserved) associated by many with the late Bill Hoole, and with good reason. It was on 23 May 1959 that Driver Hoole drove his favourite 'No. 7' up from Doncaster on a Stephenson Locomotive Society special, with every intention of going for *Mallard*'s 1938 record of 126 mph down Stoke Bank. Only the intervention of an inspector prevented the speed going over 112 mph, a post-war record for British steam, and confirmation of the A4's evergreen status.

This famous driver's last main-line trip was in fact on the 'Elizabethan', a routine up run accomplished on time with *Merlin* on 7 July. Hoole retired leaving behind a rich legacy of railway lore, such as the occasion when he made up so much time on a southbound 'Non-Stop' that a North London station-master reported him for speeding! On this particular occasion, the train had been delayed by eighty minutes by a derailment at Drem, barely twenty miles out from Edinburgh, so Hoole and his mate came through the corridor and took charge at Newcastle. This was a flexible and possibly unofficial arrangement, marred by damage to the water scoop by dipping at Muskham at too fast a speed, a water replenishment stop being necessary at Grantham. Certainly, with Hoole's retirement, the East Coast main line would become a quieter place.

The railway enthusiast press believed that 1960 would be the final year of steam-hauled, non-stop services between London and Scotland. The production 'Deltics' were scheduled to make their appearance during the year, while most of the 2,000 hp Type 4s (later Class 40) diesels had gangway doors to permit multiple coupling. It would appear to be within the realms of possibility to adapt these to form a link between locomotive and train, although the authorities may have regarded it a pointless exercise to use a type so lacking a reserve of motive power, when a 3,300 hp unit was expected in service so soon.

In fact the 'Deltics' appearance was postponed to the following year, with no accelerated timetable resulting until 1962, so the A4s carried the 'Non-Stop' tradition into the first two years of the 1960s. It all began on 13 June, with the avian pairing of *Gannet* on the down 'Elizabethan' and *Merlin* on the up; the loading was reduced by one coach due to a compression of restaurant facilities, a case of too little weight reduction, made too late.

Now preserved in the USA, No. 60008 *Dwight D. Eisenhower*, previously *Golden Shuttle*, is seen near Oakleigh Park in 1960, by which time it had been without its corridor tender for three years. (Courtney Haydon)

On the first Sunday of the summer timetable, *Merlin* slightly blemished Haymarket's fine record of service on the 'Non-Stop' when she had to be removed from the balancing up weekend service at Peterborough for an unspecified reason. It could not have been a major problem for No. 60027 went on to run up fifty-seven appearances on the 'Elizabethan' and its weekend equivalents, including forty-six consecutive journeys between 22 June and 6 August.

A footplate traveller fortunate to travel up and down between the capitals with *Merlin* during the summer reported the load as around 385/390 tons gross and time well in hand on both trips. Indeed, on the up journey, arrival at King's Cross was fifteen minutes early, the nett time being only two minutes over six hours at an average speed of 65 mph. The down journey, accomplished three minutes early in 371 minutes nett, included an uphill average speed of 72 mph over the fifteen miles from Tallington to Stoke.

The only failure on the 'Non-Stop' itself was reported to centre on No. 60032 *Gannet* on the 1 September down service. No. 60024 *Kingfisher* took the train the next day, but a Haymarket engine may have been stopped at the southern end of the journey one day in August, as there was a ten-day period when Nos. 60025/29/32 maintained the service. The final runs of the year, on 9 September, were taken by No. 60025 *Falcon* (down) and *Merlin* (up).

'Steam operation of the famous "Elizabethan" goes out in a blaze of glory.' So wrote Cecil J. Allen in *Modern Railways* after the end of the 1961 season, which was not only

Seen from the station bridge, the original A4, now BR No. 60014 *Silver Link*, passes Alne station on a Sunday, King's Cross–Edinburgh express, before being fitted with a double chimney in October 1957. (J. Davenport)

the last full summer of steam-powered non-stop operation, but, although Mr Allen was not to know it at the time, the last ever. Incredibly, or as the late Mr Allen himself might have said, *mirabile dictu*, this venerable expert's writing career spanned the entire story of the East Coast non-stops, and with something to spare before and after. 'CJA' was undoubtedly the doyen of railway journalism. He published two interesting runs from the last year of the steam-powered 'Elizabethan', which will be mentioned in due course.

The twelfth of June saw the start of the 1961 'season', with No. 60028 *Walter K. Whigham* working down on the 1A12 and No. 60031 *Golden Plover* southwards on the 1A33, to give the services their BR reporting numbers. King's Cross rostered Nos. 60014/28/30/33 during the summer, with No. 60022 *Mallard* heading the last down train. Haymarket relied on Nos. 60009/24/31, the first of these powering the last up service.

The first of the London allocation to be listed above was none other than the former LNER No. 2509 *Silver Link*. An unusual choice for the 'Elizabethan', she worked no fewer than forty services, all of twenty-six years after construction, at an age when her 'Deltic' successors would be pottering along preserved branch lines. If this seems an uncharitable comparison with locomotives which achieved an unprecedented summit of intensive utilization, it must be said that these later units brought about the premature withdrawal of this pioneer A4, surely one of the most important locomotives not to be preserved.

One slight blot on *Silver Link*'s working record occurred on 23 August when, stopped by a signal on the 1 in 78 just outside Waverley at Calton South tunnel, the Pacific was unable to restart her train. J37 No. 64591 came to the rescue; possibly the A4 had been unable to use sand to gain adhesion because of the early type of track circuiting in use. The only actual failure on the 'Elizabethan' that year featured No. 60030 *Golden Fleece*, taken off a down train at Newcastle with injector trouble, her relief being A3 No. 60040 *Cameronian*.

Despite the increasing availability of the Class 40s during 1961, not to mention the production 'Deltics' which began to appear from April onwards, the A4s almost certainly had the most difficult haulage task on the ECML that year. Such regularly diesel-hauled trains as the 'Morning Talisman' and the 'Tees Tyne Pullman' – neither of which loaded to more than 315 tons tare – were allowed $2\frac{1}{2}$ minutes more on the York–King's Cross section in the up direction than the 'Non-Stop'. Yet the 'Elizabethan's' overall punctuality appears to have been good, and Michael T. Hedderly recorded an up journey behind No. 60024 *Kingfisher* which, although completed some $1\frac{3}{4}$ minutes behind time, actually worked out at around 370 minutes nett. As C.J. Allen gave this run a detailed scrutiny in *Modern Railways*, it is worth recalling this swan-song of the 'Elizabethan'.

As *Kingfisher* pulled out of Waverley, an unwilling passenger was struggling to open a refractory carriage door and alight. This was a mother seeing her small son off southwards but who found that she was travelling with him whether she wanted to or not! When the guard learned of the unintended 'stowaway', he was able to make his way through the corridor tender to suggest to the engine crew a stop at Berwick. This, plus a slowing at Grantshouse – the first of six – put the train $3\frac{1}{2}$ minutes late into Northumberland where a further two minutes were dropped on a fairly toughly timed section. Newcastle was passed some five minutes late but good running through County Durham and a $36\frac{1}{4}$-minute dash across the 'racing stretch' meant that Driver Redpark and Fireman Lister were able to hand over to Driver Kirton and Fireman Hancox with the 'Elizabethan' only one minute late at the half-way stage.

The first A4 to head a southbound 'Non-Stop' after the Second World War was Haymarket's A4 No. 60009 *Union of South Africa* (now preserved). This engine also headed the last southbound 'Non-Stop' of all, on 9 September 1961. In this mid-1950s picture she is seen climbing towards Grantshouse with the down 'Elizabethan'. (John Robertson).

Three permanent way delays between Doncaster and Retford meant that good uphill running was necessary on the 1 in 200 climbs to Peascliffe tunnel and Stoke summit, while a maximum of 93 mph down the bank put the express back on schedule by Peterborough. A further signal check to walking pace meant that *Kingfisher* had then to produce some high speeds on the approach to London before a dead stand outside the terminus forced a slightly late arrival. In contrast to the early 'Non-Stop' days of 1928, when a momentary signal check caused 'consternation' on No. 4472's footplate, the post-war 'Elizabethan' appeared to have to accept traffic checks as an everyday fact of life. Nevertheless, the ability of the A4 and her two crews to run a near-400 ton train between the capitals all but punctually, despite six permanent way slacks, two dead stands and a serious slowing for signals, spoke volumes for the standard of staff operation.

In contrast, the down service was reportedly dogged all summer by stops for water at such locations as Darlington, Berwick and Grantshouse, apparently because an earlier train pre-empted the water-troughs at Wiske Moor and Lucker. This phantom express was probably the 'Anglo–Scottish Car Carrier' running late; it was due to pass through Berwick twenty-six minutes ahead of the 'Non-Stop'. Even so, the water-trough pumps should have been able to ensure a full pick-up. Whether the last northbound journey, on 9 September, had to make a water stop is not clear, although a photograph in the

The last steam-hauled 'Elizabethan' in the down direction approaches Joppa on 9 September 1961, with only four miles to go before the end of regular non-stop running between the capitals by Gresley Pacifics. *Mallard* has just brought her famous train under the road-bridge carrying the A1. (W.S. Sellar)

periodical press showed No. 60009 having to take water from the column at Grantshouse on a down service in late summer.

Water-troughs seem to have been unable to cope with demand in 1961, particularly at the height of the summer season, and R.A.H. Weight recorded an up journey at the end of August when this same locomotive was forced to stop for water at Grantham. There then ensued a highly-creditable 100-minute run to King's Cross, with 99 mph being touched 'down the hill' to Peterborough. The final arrival time of this much-delayed working was not recorded.

No such delay was reported on the last up service, headed by this same engine, *Union of South Africa*, and it is appropriate to close our history of the non-stop 'Elizabethan' with an account, again from the pen of Cecil J. Allen, of the later stages of an up run from this fine Pacific. This was timed by the Revd R.S. Haines who recorded that the train passed Grantham ten minutes late at 65 mph. Only 5 mph was dropped to Stoke summit and 92 mph attained down the other side. Half the deficit was made up by Peterborough – 29.1 miles from Grantham in slightly less than twenty-four minutes – but recovery was slow from the then compulsory 20 mph slack through that station. By Huntingdon 'No. 9' was really being opened up and, in the words of Mr Allen, 'the time of twenty minutes and five seconds from Huntingdon to Hitchin (twenty-seven miles) would want some beating' and made with a 380-ton gross load. Bear in mind too, that by Hitchin the A4 had already steamed for some 360 miles without a break.

Hatfield was passed on time, and even with a slow pace through the tunnels to King's

No. 4472 *Flying Scotsman* as she never was during her working life. Following preservation, this proud Pacific was decked out in 1969 with US-style whistle and bell for a forthcoming transatlantic tour, while the second tender (belonging at one time to A4 No. 60009) enabled her to repeat her pioneering 1928 non-stop run between London and Edinburgh forty years later. (Photomatic)

Cross, arrival was some two minutes to the good, in ninety-six minutes and forty-three seconds from Grantham, or ninety-three minutes nett for the 105½ miles. Again, there is ample evidence that the machines and men had something to spare, a potential that could have been put to good use by lightening the load and tightening the schedule, particularly in the years before the Potter's Bar widening.

Union of South Africa's performance was a fitting conclusion to 'Non-Stop' services across the Anglo–Scottish border. From now on, although there would be one or two such journeys yet to come, they would be in the 'stunt' category, while the configuration of certain diesel locomotives, to say nothing of the later IC125s, would permit crew-changing while in motion. Soon there was to be a dramatic schedule reduction, thanks to a massive increase of haulage power accomplished on a much improved permanent way.

The first of these stunts, although it was nevertheless a fine example of railway operation, was described at the time as the last-ever steam non-stop journey from London to Edinburgh. This was not borne out by history, but the Railway Correspondence and Travel, and Stephenson Locomotive societies deserved full marks for enterprise in organising the 'Aberdeen Flyer' for 2 June 1962.

This special was due to leave King's Cross at 8.00 a.m. with an eight-coach load on a challenging 385-minute schedule to Edinburgh. No. 60022 *Mallard* was the motive power provided, her chime whistle echoing round King's Cross as she steamed northwards. Unfortunately, a hot-box on a freight ahead of her, on the two-track section at Chathill,

Northumberland, brought the 'Flyer' to an unscheduled halt and arrival at Waverley was at 2.42 p.m. Nevertheless, a respectable time, some eighteen minutes faster than the best pre-war, non-stop schedule, although obviously made with a much lighter load.

Sister(?) engine No. 60004 *William Whitelaw* headed the special forward to Aberdeen (incidentally, King's Cross A4 No. 60015 *Quicksilver* unusually stood as reserve engine at Edinburgh) and Aberdeen was reached some five minutes early. The return journey was made via the former Caledonian and London North Western lines to Euston, where the special finally came to rest next day some three hours late. The A4s had carried out their assigned task without the slightest trouble, and another non-stop run would have been added to the list had it not been for circumstances beyond the control of *Mallard*'s crew.

All this took place sixteen days from the introduction of the accelerated 'Deltic' timetable which gave no fewer than three six-hour trains between London and Edinburgh. One of these was the 'Elizabethan', although an unadvertised stop was now made in Newcastle Central from 11.40 a.m. to 11.42 a.m. in the up direction and from 1.31½ p.m. to 1.33½ p.m. in the down. One periodical reported that medical advice had decided the BR management not to arrange for the replacement crew to travel in the rear 'Deltic' cab, while another suggested that the men had been divided on the idea. The *Railway Observer* suggested carrying on with the A4s on the new schedule; what a fascinating idea that would have been, given a lighter load!

On the day of the new timetable's introduction, No. 60103 – none other than the former No. 4472 *Flying Scotsman* – was in King's Cross station. A nice historical touch, one might think, but in fact this was an operational exigency, and, according to some enthusiasts, the A3 was deliberately moved into one of the tunnels so as not to distract the camera lenses and spoil the 'Deltics' day. Alan Pegler was later to claim that this was one of his reasons for buying the engine in the following year. Certainly, BR appears to have had no more intention of preserving her than they had *Silver Link*.

Six years were to pass, and *Flying Scotsman* came back. On 1 May 1968 No. 4472, equipped with *two* corridor tenders, prepared to mark the fortieth anniversary of the first-ever King's Cross–Waverley non-stop with a commemorative run. Witnessed by television cameras, there was a considerable element of doubt as to whether the journey was even possible at all. Only three sets of troughs remained operative – at Scrooby, Wiske Moor, and Lucker, meaning that the Pacific would have to traverse nearly 150 miles before her first replenishment. To bridge this gap a second tender – belonging incidentally to that expert proponent of post-war non-stop running, No. 60009 *Union of South Africa* – had been fitted to increase the engine's range. Nevertheless, a road water tanker had been engaged to stand by for a possible rendezvous with the train at Berwick.

At Doncaster the train was reduced to walking pace because of a broken rail, but the wheels kept turning, much to the delight of the packed complement of passengers in the seven coaches. But a red colour-light signal greeted the train on the Royal Border Bridge, where forty years previously the crew of *William Whitelaw* had anxiously scanned the skies for the pursuing *City of Glasgow*, and the brakes ominously ground on. Creeping towards the signal, it dawned on *Flying Scotsman*'s crew that the Tweedmouth signalman was putting them 'inside' in case water was needed.

The BBC film of the time shows Mr Pegler giving an impromptu press conference in the buffet car as Berwick approached, stressing that it would be the crew's decision

A BBC cameraman secures a close-up of a famous nameplate as its owner waits for the right away from King's Cross on the 'Aberdeen Flyer' on 2 June 1962. This special train attempted to run non-stop to Edinburgh (Waverley), but was foiled by a delay to a preceeding train. Another A4 Pacific took over for the following stage of the journey to Aberdeen, which was reached early. (D.A. Anderson)

whether or not to risk proceeding to Edinburgh without stopping. The locomotive's owner, sporting a Festiniog Railway cap when on the footplate, speculated that around 2,500–3,000 gallons remained in the tender after only one successful and two disappointing 'pick-ups'. This was confirmed in a close-up in the engine cab of the footplate personnel agreeing amongst themselves that they should risk pressing on, although the shot was probably edited in later, and includes no detailed discussion about the state of the locomotive at this crucial point of its historic run. After much whistling, a slow passage through the down goods yard at Berwick resulted, but at least the non-stop myth was preserved. To a ribald suggestion from a passenger that the water supply could be supplemented by bottled beer from the buffet car, Pegler confirmed that he suspected that No. 4472 could run very well on light ale!

As one might deduce from the 1951 water consumption calculations, 2,500 gallons of water proved ample for the remaining fifty-eight miles, and there were no further problems. Edinburgh was reached in approximately $7\frac{3}{4}$ hours, some thirty minutes faster than in 1928, although the load then was of course heavier. Arrival at Waverley was greeted by all the trappings of Scottish civic ceremony including bagpipes and a personal greeting from the Lord Provost.

A good Gresley engine can not only make history, it can repeat it, forty years on.

Her tender almost spilling over with coal, A4 No. 60017 *Silver Fox*, one of the original 'streamliners', leaves Haymarket depot for Waverley station to head the up 'Elizabethan' around 1958. (D.A. Anderson)

Greenwood Signal Box is the location for this view of No. 60011 *Empire of India* on the London-bound 'Capitals Limited' in September 1952. (J. Davenport)

Postscript

It would probably be premature to say that long-distance non-stop running is a figment of the past. No technical obstacle prevents Inter-City from instituting such services again, indeed distances of even more than 400 miles could be attempted. Admittedly, this would nullify one of the main advantages of diesel or electric traction, their ability to accelerate very quickly from a start, thus allowing intermediate station stops on a fast schedule.

But, in any case, non-stop running would not be the same again . . . as when a crew came on duty in mid-journey (one man at a time) by making their way through the lurching vestibule between coach and tender, then up a step and through the dimly-lit corridor, ringing with the vibration from the now-vanished rail-joints amplified by the thousands of gallons of water at the footplatemen's left shoulders. And then emerging on to the footplate which would be predictably tidy, the floor swept, the fire even and unholed to the inspection of the fresh fireman as he used his shovel to shield his gaze. Barely a sentence would be exchanged between the drivers as the incumbent vacated his bucket seat to the new man, exchanging control of a near 600-ton artefact travelling at around 70 mph, as if passing round newspapers in the mess-room. It was a phenomenon in transport operation as unique as it was simple.

For every reported incidence of failure, of inability to overcome time lost to checks, of damaged water scoops causing a water shortage, there were a dozen uneventful, punctual runs now lost to memory.

For every immortal, much-publicized record set up by *Silver Link* or *Mallard*, there was an unknown number of marvellous runs by the perennial stalwarts on the East Coast 'Non-Stop' – *Seagull*, *Merlin* and *Union of South Africa* in particular.

As long as mankind has affection for the machines he has created, they will be remembered.

Bibliography

Books

Brown, F.A.S. *Nigel Gresley*. Ian Allan.
Coster, P.J. *In* Clay, J.F. (ed.) *Essays in Steam*. D & C, 1971.
Dow, George. *British Steam Horses*. Phoenix House, 1950.
   The East Coast Route. Locomotive Publishing, 1951.
Haresnape, B. *British Rail 1948–83; A Journey by Design*. Ian Allan, 1983.
Hoole, K. *The East Coast Main Line Since 1925*. Ian Allan, 1977.
Hughes, G. *LNER*. Malaga Books, 1986.
McKillop, N. *Enginemen Elite*. Ian Allan.
Nock, O.S. *LMS Steam*. D & C, 1971.
   Main Lines Across the Border. Nelson, 1960.
   Speed Records on Britain's Railways. D & C, 1971.
Railway Correspondence & Travel Society. *Locomotives of the LNER, Part 2A*.
Rowledge, J.W.P. and Reed, B. *The Stanier 4–6–0s of the LMS*. D & C.
Semmens, P.W.B. *Engineman Extraordinary*. Ian Allan, 1966.
Townend, P. *East Coast Pacifics at Work*. Ian Allan.
Webster, H.C. *2750, Legend of a Locomotive*. Nelson, 1953.

Periodicals

BR Magazine
LMS Magazine
LNER Magazine
Modern Railways
Railway Gazette
Railway Magazine
Trains Illustrated

The author wishes to express his thanks to the staff of the Public Record Office, Scottish Record Office, National Railway Museum, National Library of Scotland, Edinburgh City Libraries and the Mitchell Library, Glasgow, particularly Murdoch Nicolson. For help with photographs the author is indebted to Kevin Robertson, W.S. Sellar, D.A. Anderson, J.T. Inglis and John Robertson.

Appendices

LNER LOCOMOTIVES ON LONDON—EDINBURGH NON-STOP WORKINGS

(Arranged chronologically and then by LNER Number)

LNER No.	BR No.	Class	Original Name	Re-named	Summer Available for Non-Stop First	Last
2546	60047	A1	*Donovan*	–	1928	1928
2547	60048	A1	*Doncaster*	–	"	1932
2552	60053	A1	*Sansovino*	–	"	1928
2556	60057	A1	*Ormonde*	–	"	1928
2563	60064	A1	*William Whitelaw*	*Tagalie*	"	1934
2564	60065	A1	*Knight of the Thistle*	*Knight of Thistle*	"	1935
2569	60070	A1	*Gladiateur*	–	"	1928
2573	60074	A3	*Harvester*	–	"	"
2580	60081	A3	*Shotover*	–	"	"
2743	60089	A3	*Felstead*	–	"	"
2744	60090	A3	*Grand Parade*	–	"	1929
2745	60091	A3	*Captain Cuttle*	–	"	1928
4472	60103	A1	*Flying Scotsman*	–	"	1936
4475	60106	A1	*Flying Fox*	–	"	1934
4476	60107	A1	*Royal Lancer*	–	"	1936
2566	60067	A1	*Ladas*	–	1929	1929
2746	60092	A3	*Fairway*	–	1930	1936
2750	60096	A3	*Papyrus*	–	"	1937
2795	60099	A3	*Call Boy*	–	"	1936
2796	60100	A3	*Spearmint*	–	"	1936
10000	60700	W1	–	–	"	1939
4474	60105	A1	*Victor Wild*	–	1933	1934
2508	60043	A3	*Brown Jack*	–	1935	1936
2509	60014	A4	*Silver Link*	–	1936	1961
2510	60015	A4	*Quicksilver*	–	"	"
2511	60016	A4	*Silver King*	–	"	1939
2512	60017	A4	*Silver Fox*	–	"	1961
4482	60023	A4	*Golden Eagle*	–	1937	1939
4483	60024	A4	*Kingfisher*	–	"	1961
4484	60025	A4	*Falcon*	–	"	"
4485	60026	A4	*Kestrel*	*Miles Beevor*	"	1952
4486	60027	A4	*Merlin*	–	"	1961

LNER No.	BR No.	Class	Original Name	Re-named	Summer Available for Non-Stop First	Last
4487	60028	A4	*Sea Eagle*	*Walter K. Whigham*	"	"
4488	60009	A4	*Union of South Africa*	–	"	"
4489	60010	A4	*Woodcock*	*Dominion of Canada*	"	"
4490	60011	A4	*Empire of India*	–	"	"
4491	60012	A4	*Commonwealth of Australia*	–	"	"
4492	60013	A4	*Dominion of New Zealand*	–	"	. "
4493	60029	A4	*Woodcock*	–	"	"
4494	60003	A4	*Osprey*	*Andrew K. McCosh*	"	1955
4495	60030	A4	*Great Snipe*	*Golden Fleece*	"	1961
4496	60008	A4	*Golden Shuttle*	*Dwight D. Eisenhower*	"	1956
4497	60031	A4	*Golden Plover*	–	1938	1961
4498	60007	A4	*Sir Nigel Gresley*	–	"	"
4462	60004	A4	*Great Snipe*	*William Whitelaw*	1948	"
4468	60022	A4	*Mallard*	–	"	"
4902	60033	A4	*Seagull*	–	"	"
4903	60034	A4	*Peregrine*	*Lord Faringdon*	"	"
4466	60006	A4	*Herring Gull*	*Sir Ralph Wedgwood*	1950	1953
4900	60032	A4	*Gannet*	–	1954	1961
4467	60021	A4	*Wild Swan*	–	1957	"

The LNER re-numberings of 1946–8 are ignored here. The first of them was very short-lived; the second was incorporated into BR re-numbering.

NUMBER OF NON-STOP RUNS (INC. WEEKEND EQUIVALENTS) BY INDIVIDUAL LOCOMOTIVES PER YEAR

Total.	Consecutive (if known)	Loco		Depot	Year	Ref.
73+	65	60012	*Commonwealth of Australia*	Hay.	1957	1
62	–	60027	*Merlin*	Hay.	1959	2
62	52	4492	*Dominion of New Zealand*	KX	1937	3
61	38	60009	*Union of South Africa*	Hay.	1954	4
57	46	60027	*Merlin*	Hay.	1960	5
57	–	60011	*Empire of India*	Hay.	1956	6
56	–	60033	*Seagull*	KX	1956	7
53	–	60028	*Walter K. Whigham*	KX	1959	8
50	–	60033	*Seagull*	KX	1955	9
42	28	60027	*Merlin*	Hay.	1952	10
40	–	60014	*Silver Link*	KX	1961	11

References:

1. *Trains Illustrated* (TI), Nov. 1957, p. 619.
2. *Railway Observer* (RO), 1959, p. 303.
3. RCTS History (see Bibliography), Vol. 2A, pp. 124–5. The same source suggests, on p. 224, that this locomotive was transferred from KX to Haymarket during this summer.
4. TI, 1954, p. 488.

5. RO, 1960, p. 359. The RCTS, 2A, p. 131 credits this engine with no fewer than seventy-four non-stop trips during 1960, something not borne out by the magazine published at the time by the same society.
6. RO, Oct. 1956; TI 1956, p. 595. This locomotive was believed to have been removed from the service because of the floods emergency on 28 August; otherwise it might have attained an even higher figure.
7. TI, 1956, p. 575.
8. RO, 1959, p. 303.
9. TI, 1955, p. 482 – described as having made '50 round trips' (sic).
10. Semmens, P.W.B. *Bill Hoole, Engineman Extraordinary*.
11. RCTS. 2A, p. 95.

The above table is based on unofficial calculations made from published information. The author has compiled it in good faith as it certainly indicates the extent to which locomotives were under-utilized pre-war, with only one endurance record from that period, as well as the considerable improvement made possible for Gresley locomotives by technical modifications in the 1950s.

NUMBER OF NON-STOP RUNS OVER A RECORD DISTANCE, 1948

SOUTHBOUND

Date	Locomotive		Drivers (Hay)	(KX)
Aug. 24	60029	*Woodcock*	Stevenson	Brown
26	60028	*Walter K. Whigham*	Stevenson	Brown
28	60029		Stevenson	Moore
Sept. 7	60029		Swan	King
9	60029		Swan	King
11	60012	*Commonwealth of Australia*	Swan	Jarrett
15	60022	*Mallard*	Swan	Burgess
17	60029		Swan	Brown
18	60012		McLeod	King

NORTHBOUND

Date	Locomotive		Drivers (Hay)	(KX)
Aug. 25	60028		Stevenson	Brown
26	60027	*Merlin*	McLeod	King
27	60029		Stevenson	Moore
Sept. 2	60029		Stevenson	Moore
6	60029		Swan	King
7	60012		McLeod	Jarrett
8	60029		Swan	King
9	60031	*Golden Plover*	Prinkley	McLeod

Source: O.S. Nock. *The Gresley Pacifics*. David & Charles.

CHRONOLOGY OF BRITISH RECORD NON-STOP RUNS AND SERVICES

Year	Company	From	To	Distance	Comments
1873	GNR	King's Cross	Grantham	105	
1896	GWR	Paddington	Exeter	193½	Summer service
1903	LNWR	Euston	Carlisle	299	One return journey
1904	GWR	Paddington	Plymouth	245½	Reduced to 225¾ in 1906
1906?	GWR	Paddington	Fishguard	265?	Specials
1927	LNER	King's Cross	Newcastle	268	Summer service
1927	LMS	Euston	Carlisle	299	
1928	LMS	Euston	Edinburgh	400	One journey only
1928	LMS	Euston	Glasgow	401	One journey only
1928	LNER	King's Cross	Edinburgh	393	Summer service
1929	LMS	Glenboig	Euston	395½	One journey only
1936	LMS	Euston	Glasgow	401	One return journey
1948	BR	King's Cross	Edinburgh	408½	Seventeen journeys
1949	BR	Euston	Glasgow	401	One journey only

LONGEST WORLD NON-STOP RUNS OVER 390 MILES

Distance (in miles)	Date	Operator	Between	Freq.	Ref.
1017.2	23.10.36	CB&Q (USA)	Chicago–Denver	1	1
1015	26.5.34	CB&Q (USA)	Denver–Chicago	1	2
448	1876?	Penn. (USA)	Philadelphia–Pittsburgh	1	3
408.6	8/9.48	BR	Edinburgh–London	17	4
401	27.4.28	LMS	London–Glasgow	1	5
401	16/17.11.36	LMS	London–Glasgow (and return)	2	6
401	1.6.49	BR	London–Glasgow	1	7
399.75	27.4.28	LMS	London–Edinburgh	1	8
395.5	19.7.29	LMS	Glenboig–London	1	9
393	1928–39, 48–61	LNER/BR	London–Edinburgh (And vice-versa)	All summer	

References:

1. *Railway Gazette*, Vol. 66, 1937, p. 573. Log of run.
2. Ibid. Vol. 60, 1934, pp. 983 & 1085.
3. *Locomotive, Carriage & Wagon Review*. Vol. 35. 1928, p. 182. Theatrical special.
4. Apparently first mentioned in *BR Magazine* (E.NE. & Sc Regs edition) 1948, p. 266. See also *Railway Magazine* Vol. 95, 1949, p. 117.
5. *The Times*. 28 April 1928.
6. *Railway Gazette*. Vol. 64, 1936, p. 834.
7. *Railway Magazine*. Vol. 95, 1949, p. 296. Believed to be longest diesel-powered run in British rail history.
8. *The Scotsman*. 28 April 1928.
9. *Railway Magazine*. Vol. 65, 1929, p. 233.

LONDON (KING'S CROSS)—EDINBURGH (WAVERLEY) NON-STOP TIMINGS, 1928—39 AND 1948—61.

1928	8 hrs 15 mins	1937	7 hrs	1953	6 hrs 45 mins
1929	"	1938	"	1954	6 hrs 30 mins
1930	"	1939	"	1955	"
1931	"			1956	"
1932	7 hrs 30 mins	1948	7 hrs 50 mins	1957	6 hrs 35 mins
1933	"	1949	8hrs	1958	"
1934	"	1950	8hrs	1959	"
1935	"	1951	7 hrs 20 mins	1960	"
1936	7 hrs 15 mins	1952	7 hrs. 6 mins	1961	"

LNER/BR NUMBER INDEX

2500	60035	2558	60059	2599	60088	4477	60108
2501	60036	2560	60061	2743	60089	4478	60109
2502	60037	2561	60062	2744	60090	4479	60110
2503	60038	2562	60063	2745	60091	4480	60111
2504	60039	2563	60064	2746	60092	4481	60112
2505	60040	2564	60065	2747	60093	4482	60023
2506	60041	2565	60066	2748	60094	4483	60024
2507	60042	2566	60067	2749	60095	4484	60025
2508	60043	2567	60068	2750	60096	4485	60026
2509	60014	2568	60069	2751	60097	4486	60027
2510	60015	2569	60070	2752	60098	4487	60028
2511	60016	2570	60071	2795	60099	4488	60009
2512	60017	2571	60072	2796	60100	4489	60010
2543	60044	2572	60073	2797	60101	4490	60011
2544	60045	2573	60074	4462	60004	4491	60012
2545	60046	2574	60075	4463	60018	4492	60013
2546	60047	2575	60076	4464	60019	4493	60029
2547	60048	2576	60077	4465	60020	4494	60003
2548	60049	2577	60078	4466	60006	4495	60030
2549	60050	2578	60079	4467	60021	4496	60008
2550	60051	2579	60080	4468	60022	4497	60031
2551	60052	2580	60081	4470	60113	4498	60007
2552	60053	2581	60082	4471	60102	4499	60002
2553	60054	2582	60083	4472	60103	4500	60001
2554	60055	2595	60084	4473	60104	4900	60032
2555	60056	2596	60085	4474	60105	4901	60005
2556	60057	2597	60086	4475	60106	4902	60033
2557	60058	2598	60087	4476	60107	4903	60034

BR/LNER NUMBER INDEX

60001	4500	60030	4495	60059	2558	60088	2599
60002	4499	60031	4497	60060	2559	60089	2743
60003	4494	60032	4900	60061	2560	60090	2744
60004	4462	60033	4902	60062	2561	60091	2745
60005	4901	60034	4903	60063	2562	60092	2746
60006	4466	60035	2500	60064	2563	60093	2747
60007	4498	60036	2501	60065	2564	60094	2748
60008	4496	60037	2502	60066	2565	60095	2749
60009	4488	60038	2503	60067	2566	60096	2750
60010	4489	60039	2504	60068	2567	60097	2751
60011	4490	60040	2505	60069	2568	60098	2752
60012	4491	60041	2506	60070	2569	60099	2795
60013	4492	60042	2507	60071	2570	60100	2796
60014	2509	60043	2508	60072	2571	60101	2797
60015	2510	60044	2543	60073	2572	60102	4471
60016	2511	60045	2544	60074	2573	60103	4472
60017	2512	60046	2545	60075	2574	60104	4473
60018	4463	60047	2546	60076	2575	60105	4474
60019	4464	60048	2547	60077	2576	60106	4475
60020	4465	60049	2548	60078	2577	60107	4476
60021	4467	60050	2549	60079	2578	60108	4477
60022	4468	60051	2550	60080	2579	60109	4478
60023	4482	60052	2551	60081	2580	60110	4479
60024	4483	60053	2552	60082	2581	60111	4480
60025	4484	60054	2553	60083	2582	60112	4481
60026	4485	60055	2554	60084	2595	60113	4470
60027	4486	60056	2555	60085	2596		
60028	4487	60057	2556	60086	2597	60700	10000
60029	4493	60058	2557	60087	2598		

Index

Figures in *italics* relate to illustrations